Educating Today's Overindulged Youth

Combat Narcissism by Building Foundations, Not Pedestals

Chad Mason and Karen Brackman

Rowman & Littlefield Education
A division of
ROWMAN & LITTLEFIELD PUBLISHERS, INC.
Lanham • New York • Toronto • Plymouth, UK

Published by Rowman & Littlefield Education
A division of Rowman & Littlefield Publishers, Inc.
A wholly owned subsidiary of The Rowman & Littlefield Publishing Group, Inc.
4501 Forbes Boulevard, Suite 200, Lanham, Maryland 20706
http://www.rowmaneducation.com

Estover Road, Plymouth PL6 7PY, United Kingdom

Copyright © 2009 by Chad Mason and Karen Brackman

All rights reserved. No part of this book may be reproduced in any form or by any electronic or mechanical means, including information storage and retrieval systems, without written permission from the publisher, except by a reviewer who may quote passages in a review.

British Library Cataloguing in Publication Information Available

Library of Congress Cataloging-in-Publication Data

Mason, Chad, 1971-
  Educating today's overindulged youth : combat narcissism by building foundations, not pedestals / Chad Mason and Karen Brackman.
    p. cm.
  Includes bibliographical references.
  ISBN 978-1-60709-205-6 (cloth : alk. paper)—ISBN 978-1-60709-206-3 (pbk. : alk. paper)—ISBN 978-1-60709-207-0 (electronic)
  1. Education—United States. 2. Narcissism in children—United States. 3. Narcissism in adolescence—United States. I. Brackman, Karen Ann, 1965- II. Title.
  LA210.M345 2009
  371.801'9—dc22

                                                          2009015180

⊗ ™ The paper used in this publication meets the minimum requirements of American National Standard for Information Sciences—Permanence of Paper for Printed Library Materials, ANSI/NISO Z39.48-1992.

Printed in the United States of America

Contents

Acknowledgments

Thank you Carrie and Drew for your patience and support and to Stephanie for the chance to get "my time" back.

C.M.

Thanks Craig, Lauren, and Spencer for putting up with my need to chase another dream. I realize the months of time devoted to this project took away from our family time. Thanks for your patience and support. Your turn.

K.B.

~

Foreword

Theodore J. Kowalski, Kuntz Family Chair in Educational Administration, University of Dayton

The importance of educator relations with students and parents is framed by two realities. First, positive relationships are associated with student academic and social growth; as an example, parental involvement with schools frequently has been found to improve student learning. Second, stakeholder economic and political support has become essential to school improvement at the local level. Despite these realities, administrators and teachers often find it difficult to build and maintain trusting associations with others.

Though many factors affect human relations, our disposition toward conflict is arguably one of the most important. Unfortunately, many educators were socialized to believe that conflict is always a negative condition to be avoided. So when teachers and administrators are forced to interact with persons, they often avoid students who have the greatest problems and parents who are confrontational or otherwise disagreeable. This behavior is counterproductive because conflict is a natural part of collective human experience and a catalyst for positive change. Thus in the realm of effective schools, educators seek to understand, work with, and help persons who previously were ignored. Over the past few decades, pressures to improve schools at the local level and expanded knowledge of high-performing schools have incrementally caused us to change our thinking about relationships with students and parents.

This book by Chad Mason and Karen Brackman constitutes a unique contribution to the literature on educator relations. It examines student and parent narcissism and explains why and how this trait can be dysfunctional and a deterrent to student learning. The authors address this topic from a perspective of their collective experiences in schools. Their informal yet highly relevant analysis provides insights that educators will find beneficial. Moreover, they provide examples to fortify their positions about recognizing and dealing with narcissism.

Recently, the American Psychological Association reported that one in five adults has a personality disorder. Arguably, narcissism, when sufficiently excessive, is one of the most common. The condition, as explained in this book, can affect student social and academic growth in a myriad of ways. Clearly then, educators need to understand this condition and its severity; and they must be able to apply their knowledge to modify behavior so that students can be more successful. Mason and Brackman not only detail the nature and effects of self-absorption, but they also offer practical interventions for counteracting it.

In summary, this is a useful book for both administrators and teachers because it addresses a growing problem in the context of contemporary social issues. The content broadens our knowledge of human behavior and our understanding of how negative behavior attenuates both student learning and school effectiveness. Indirectly, the content also encourages us to reflect about our own behavior—most notably to assess our personality traits and to ponder the extent to which they are positive or negative forces in relationship building.

~

Preface

Many of the ideas for this book began as informal discussions with various members of the education profession, and over time these discussions prompted serious concerns on the topic of narcissism and dealing with self-absorbed students, parents, and even fellow educators. This book is meant to call attention to these concerns—specifically, to the direction education has been going for some time and the negative effects of that course if substantial changes are not made—both for the sake of the nation's school children and the thousands of dedicated professionals in the educational arena. Through extensive reading, nearly thirty-five years of combined educational experience, and sound observation and reflection, we have set out to tackle the growing problem of narcissism in education.

A colleague once stated, "There just do not seem to be any rules anymore." Initially, this statement appeared to be misleading and inaccurate, as, in fact, more rules exist than *ever* before. School handbooks are growing thicker each year, and school officials are forced to address issues that many would never have dreamed of decades ago. Nonetheless, this colleague's statement took on an essence of truth as we began to explore the complexities of narcissism and its related sense of entitlement. Rules exist. However, no rules exist without exceptions *and* the option to be circumvented. Getting past rules may occur through excessive demands, self-justifying excuses, or even lying—all hallmarks of narcissistic, self-absorbed behavior. In actuality, if education continues on its current path of trying to accommodate every unique situation of its population, the "rule book" will in fact have more pages than an OSHA handbook. But none of the rules will apply to all.

Another concern regarding education is that many educators are becoming disheartened and apathetic towards the career. Educational employee turnover has a significant cost to the American taxpayer in terms of dollars and cents—and an even greater significance to the student when a quality teacher is no longer in the classroom.

Many studies have been conducted to examine why teachers leave the profession, and two answers seem to surface with each report—lack of respect and lack of administrative support. As we examined the task of educating students in today's climate and engaged in dialogue with our peers, we were determined to evaluate what "lack of respect" and "lack of administrative support" *looks* like. How do these concepts manifest themselves in the day-to-day life of a teacher? In many ways, these concepts appear to go hand-in-hand. An ever-increasing lack of respect by the students, their parents, and society at large is on the rise. Further, staff members, in general, appear to believe that the administration does not support their attempts to take a professional stand.

Many school personnel may find themselves in situations where their ability, character, or expertise is called into question. As the respect for the profession steadily decreases, we set out to examine how students and parents justify second-guessing and questioning the expertise of school personnel on a regular basis. What mindsets and attitudes lead to such behaviors? Our examination continually led to the central characteristics and personality traits of narcissism, and, resoundingly, numerous facets of the American lifestyle were found to reflect these traits.

Decades ago, the self-esteem movement began in California, and the mindset of the American individual altered considerably. As a result, the educational ranks have suffered in many ways. To date, nearly 15,000 publications have been written on promoting self and the importance of a child's self-esteem in learning and success in life. Lost in this approach are the sincerity necessary for *true* self-esteem and the feelings of good old-fashioned hard work.

As you read through this publication and explore the topic of narcissism and over-indulgence, we encourage collegial discussion and debate. If this book inspires research, further examination of the topic, or even half the number of publications that were written on self-esteem, this project has been a successful venture.

Finally, it is our sincere hope that one approaches this topic with reflection and the same careful observation with which it was written. If school personnel do not begin to "take back" the school setting and the prestige that should come with formal education, the consequences for the profession, our children, and our society may be severe.

CHAPTER ONE

~

A Narcissistic Society

Long ago in Greek folklore, a myth evolved regarding a character by the name of Narcissus. Legend has it that Narcissus was an extremely good-looking and beautiful specimen of a man. In fact, his beauty was so great that he was unable to find a mate considered suitable to him and worthy of his beauty and stature. As punishment for shunning and breaking the hearts of so many, a spell was cast on Narcissus so that he would know the pain of unrequited love.

According to the tale, he awoke one day next to a stream and discovered the most beautiful image he had ever beheld in the surface of the water—that of his own reflection. Unknowingly, he was so taken by the beautiful image that he spent many of his remaining days adoring it—thinking it was a beautiful woman. He frequently reached into the water to touch the woman, but each time the image would disappear into the rippling water. As historian and social critic Christopher Lasch (1979) interprets the mythological tale, Narcissus had not only vainly fallen in love with himself, but he also had failed to distinguish between himself and his surroundings, as he was completely self-absorbed. As the story goes, this self-absorption eventually ended in great unhappiness and human demise for Narcissus.

Over time, in accordance with the myth, the name *Narcissus* became synonymous with the vanity and self-indulgence the main character displayed. Today, references to Narcissus, or the generalized term *narcissism*, have become even more prevalent and broader in meaning. Narcissism does not merely incorporate self-admiration; it also implies a particular *mindset* of an individual, a group, or even a culture. This mindset carries with it a certain way people feel they should be perceived by others; a certain way they feel they should be treated by others; and a certain way they should, in return, appropriately respond to the treatment of others. In general, this mindset incorporates several traits that result in a self-centered, self-indulgent, hedonistic way of thinking and living.

Especially since the 1970s, numerous studies and works on narcissism and its effects on various aspects of American society have been published. In fact, one could read excerpts from Lasch's work *The Culture of Narcissism: American Life in an Age of Diminishing Expectations*, published in 1979, and realize the traits of Americans he scorned in the 1970s still persevere—with greater strength—in the current culture of the United States:

> The psychological patterns associated with pathological narcissism, . . . in less exaggerated form manifest themselves in so many patterns of American culture—in the fascination with fame and celebrity, the fear of competition, the inability to suspend disbelief, the shallowness and transitory quality of personal relations. (p. 176)

Further, he goes on to explain that American "society reinforces these patterns not only through 'indulgent education' and general permissiveness but through advertising, demand creation, and the mass culture of hedonism" (p. 180).

As suggested by Lasch (1979), narcissism appears to afflict those in a consumer-driven society—as, of course, the United States is—more than other cultures and countries. This is not to imply that other societies do not have vain or conceited individuals; they do. It also is not to imply that a consumer-driven society cannot have altruistic, selfless individuals; it can. However, narcissism's effects appear to more significantly hamper a society that perpetually inundates its citizens with products emphasizing an individual's looks or appearance and equating possession of these and other products with self-worth. Arguably, one would potentially not receive much debate in listing the United States as one of the most vain and narcissistic cultures in the world today. Examples of narcissism of varying degrees surround us.

Several years ago, we were fortunate enough to listen to educational psychologist John Rosemond speak regarding parenting and the education of today's youth. One portion of his speech particularly impacted us in how it related to the topic of narcissism. It was in regard to the plethora of educational bumper stickers attached to many vehicles across the country. Many such advertisements make the claim or statement in one form or another, "My child is an honor student at *Anyschool* U.S.A." His position simply stated that no self-respecting parent would have had such an item on a car forty years ago; doing so was an example of bragging and would have been considered an example of a person lacking proper etiquette. While it is a huge leap to blame many of today's problems on bumper stickers, it is a sign of what is becoming a systemic and cultural problem afflicting our country—an unbalanced focus on *self*.

Similarly, in some youth sporting leagues, rather than handing out a traditional trophy to recognize outstanding player accomplishments, athletes are given T-shirts to wear advertising their individual successes. The T-shirt may read "Most Valuable Player" or "Best Defensive Player" across the back. It is healthy to feel proud of achievements, but where have the age-old lessons of humility and learning to not flaunt successes gone?

The advertisement world also reeks of self-indulgence. In one regard, Americans are slaves to a toxic consumerism—we *must* have "stuff" and lots of it! Many Americans simply live to do what feels good at the time and strive to take advantage of all that comes with the "good life." Much of what the media highlights showcases glamorous lifestyles, famous celebrities, and wealth, which enables catered living with an enormous sense of entitlement.

In fact, in the *New York Times* bestseller *Made to Stick: Why Some Ideas Survive and Others Die*, Chip and Dan Heath (2007) attempt to pinpoint why some advertising campaigns resonate so well with the American people. One of the hallmark characteristics of successful advertisement is the ability to appeal to the consumers' emotions and to their *self*-interests. It is not surprising, then, in a country that is inundated with advertising (and much appealing to our self-interest) that it has some effect on the American psyche.

Our culture is bombarded with commercials, advertising, and public messages offering what we as Americans *deserve* and *need* to be truly happy. Unfortunately, these messages are not always received in a healthy way. Young girls are particularly vulnerable to the effects of a consumer-driven culture. Anorexia, bulimia, depression, and anxiety are just a few of the by-products of growing up in a culture that encourages constant self-evaluation and the rush to meet an unrealistic sense of perfection. Having said this, to lay all the blame at the feet of those in the media is naïve and irresponsible; however, those in the media must admit they do indeed play a role in developing narcissistic attitudes.

Another important topic to examine is the number of Americans—and even entire industries—who financially profit from fostering the narcissistic characteristics of our culture. As noted earlier, advertising executives perpetually shower their audiences with the need to be pretty, smart, slim, happy, or more physically fit; and, of course, they profit when Americans indulge.

Attorneys and legal experts seek out clients to bring litigation against those who have wronged them and make the accused pay a heavy penance for their transgressions. Pharmaceutical companies encourage people to think of themselves with campaigns that encourage self-reflection and fear, "You may have this and not even know it," or "Improve your appearance with this tiny pill—no physical effort required." The entertainment industry glamorizes those living the high life and all the material goods that accompany their successes.

Further, politicians and public servants also take advantage of a narcissistic mindset. Think how often a candidate running for office has based his or her platform on a narcissistic soft spot: "You need to elect me because my predecessor did not come through for *you!*" The election industry is based on describing what we, as Americans, deserve (are entitled to) and how a particular political candidate promises to provide for society. Most importantly, as we focus much of this book on education, politicians use children, test scores, and learning as ammunition in this ongoing political battle. The results for those of us in the ranks each day can be oppressive and potentially devastating.

Fortunately for these profiting groups (and others), they can continually benefit from our self-absorbed, narcissistic culture due to one of the basic characteristics of the human psyche. The "attention cup" of a narcissist can never be totally full. A common personality trait in many narcissistic individuals is the never-ending hunger for self-gratification, control, attention, or peer feedback. The narcissist quickly drains energy and resources from the larger group whether that group is in the workplace, with the family, at a social gathering, or in the classroom. These individuals are "on stage" and demand and deserve (in their eyes) constant attention or approval.

As the narcissist is forever looking for the spotlight, recent advances in technology have enabled the self-absorbed to enjoy avenues to further receive this attention. Internet Websites such as YouTube, MySpace, Facebook, and other sites, which allow individuals to post personal pictures, video, and commentary, top the list of the most frequently visited locations. These sites have made "stardom" seem more accessible and available, making *substantive talent* less important in obtaining fame and celebrity status.

Further, television programs that fall in the "reality television" genre took the country by storm within the last decade. *Survivor, Big Brother, The Amazing Race, American Idol,* and others promoted the idea of the "average Joe" experiencing television fame and instantly struck a chord in the minds of millions of Americans. Many people felt as though they could relate to those on the television and believed, "I am as good, smart, pretty, or talented as he or she is—I could be on this show!"

As indicated by the title of this publication, this project was completed to identify the individual characteristics of citizens in a narcissistic culture and examine how those characteristics affect the educational system in a larger societal context. As overindulgence and narcissism have been an issue in much of American culture for some time, today's education system appears to be overwhelmed by the harmful effects associated with this topic.

Do bumper stickers, media promotions, politicians, reality TV, and social-networking Websites affect narcissism and relate to the field of education? Are these topics important to discuss when training the future classroom teachers responsible for educating the American child? The answer to both of these questions is quite simply a resounding, Yes!

In examining one particular example of "reality TV," one may begin to understand just how these examples symbolize the inherent difficulties in teaching narcissistic children and working with their parents. The television show *American Idol* is a large-scale singing show where contestants perform for a panel of celebrity judges in order to become the last person standing in a vote of the American people. One of the judges, Simon Cowell, is known for being brutally honest and harsh in his criticism of the contestants.

Many group discussions regarding the popular television show usually provide an opportunity for one member to prompt, "Do those people really think they are talented?" Quite honestly, the answer on most occasions is yes, they do. In spite of how poor a performer they may be, many contestants are visibly hostile at being dismissed from the show—particularly if they have received criticism from Simon Cowell regarding their lack of talent. It makes one wonder if Mr. Cowell's criticism may in fact be the *first* that some of these contestants have encountered, thus exacerbating the harshness of his words. We do not support degrading a person's character for a lack of singing talent, but honestly critiquing a person's singing talent in a voluntary singing audition is rather fair. Some of the failing contestants seem appalled that this indeed is the process for qualifying for the show.

In what we term the *American Idol* Reality-Check, it is possible to begin to delineate the parallel between Simon Cowell as a talent judge and the American teacher. In some ways, the criticism/feedback aspect of the show is symbolic of how educating today's youth and the repercussions from their parents is, at times, tumultuous. In a narcissistic culture, the judge's credibility is immediately called into question—even if he or she has the experience and expertise necessary to fill the position. Likewise, today's teacher must understand that more and more students and their parents challenge evaluative statements, and the teacher's expertise may immediately be questioned.

Look around—positions that were once revered no longer have their status in American society. Teachers, doctors, clergy, police, fire officials—the list goes on. Regardless of the level of education, the mentality of the general public seems to be—"I am just as good as you!" What if they aren't? Job training, education, and expertise lose merit when a narcissistic culture encourages the perception that *those people* (the professionals) are no better than anyone else. We are not talking about self-worth or personal value in this context, but when dealing with trained professionals, so many believe that their opinions should have equal value or even override that of the experts. Many professions have felt the sting of loss of credibility from this self-absorbed, narcissistic notion.

The effects of this are becoming apparent in schools, as some educators simply are shying away from putting students in situations where they could be rated, criticized, or evaluated for fear of retribution. For example, Bounds reports that Boulder Valley School District has stopped the practice of utilizing grade point averages in determining student rank and ultimately valedictorians to eliminate "unhealthy competition" (2007, p. 2). Under their new system, more students are able to be recognized as being at the top of the class.

Also, some schools no longer use red ink when grading student work, as the "shock" of red ink can be too detrimental in the growth of a child's self-esteem. Even more, Schenker (2007) wrote an article on the perception a group of parents had of whether or not their children had a good teacher; student "satisfaction" over increased academic achievement was the ultimate factor in determining if a child had a quality teacher for the majority of these parents.

In some respects, even *constructive* criticism is now viewed as unprofessional conduct, lowering self-esteem and demeaning a child's fragile psyche. Indeed, many narcissistic parents have posed the question, "How dare you attempt to quell my child's dream?" Further, as many narcissistic parents live vicariously through their children, any educational criticism of a child is possibly viewed as a personal attack on a parent's abilities both as a parent and also as a judge of his or her child's strengths.

To an extreme, these parenting concerns are commonly referred to as *overindulgence* rather than *narcissism*. In that respect, the title of this book could be misleading, as overindulgence and narcissism, by definition, are not the same. Typically, overindulgence denotes a showering of attention, material goods, time, effort, or energy on another individual; in contrast, narcissism denotes an excessive focus on self. Nevertheless, in terms of their correlating effects, the terms are impossible to separate. In short, repeatedly overindulging an individual often conditions that person to begin to expect the time, effort, or materials he has become accustomed to receiving. Thus, overindulgence often leads to the effects of the overriding umbrella of narcissism.

As educators find themselves facing these narcissistic views more and more on the job, this publication was written to encourage reflection on interactions with students and parents. Most assuredly, many student, parent, and even some colleague "faces" will come to mind in reading the topics presented. It is also helpful for educators to examine their educational styles, their role in the climate of their building, and their communication techniques. Ultimately, the goal in bringing attention to this topic is to provide solace in the face of those who can drain the creative and emotional resources of individuals in charge of educating today's youth.

CHAPTER TWO

~

Narcissism Defined

Chapter One depicts some casual observations of narcissism in America. In citing these illustrations, it is extremely important that these claims are not taken as mere complaints from "some frustrated educators." In fact, narcissism, along with other related conditions, has been widely recognized, researched, and written about for several decades.

Karnick (2007) shares one particular study that measures narcissism in college students from 1982–2006. The researchers, led by Professor Jean Twenge of San Diego State University, asked 16,475 college students across the nation to respond to statements on a standardized Narcissistic Personality Inventory (NPI). It included such items as the following:

"If I ruled the world, it would be a better place."
"I think I am a special person."
"I can live my life any way I want to." (Karnick, 2007, p. 1)

The responses were mathematically computed and statistically compared. The results of the study show that the students' NPI scores consistently increased from the initial testing from 1982 through 2006. In fact, two-thirds of the college students in 2006 had above-average scores on the NPI, which is a thirty-percent increase from the scores in 1982.

Karnick (2007) explains that the authors of this research feel these results could have several negative implications for America, including a lack of quality relationships among people, a lack of compassion and empathy toward others, and an excessive focus on self. The researchers directly correlate the narcissistic trend in society to the self-esteem movements of the 1980s and also agree narcissism can be fostered through such technology media as MySpace and YouTube.

Another major recognition of growing narcissism in America was the addition of narcissistic personality disorder (NPD) to the *Diagnostic and Statistical Manual of Mental Disorders* (DSM) in 1980. As defined by PSYweb. com in the article "DSM-IV Multiaxial System (Made Easy)," the DSM is "the standardized classification of mental disorders used by mental health professionals in the United States." Thus it provides thorough information on precisely defining narcissism, or specifically NPD.

The DSM IV describes NPD as an affliction that surfaces by early adulthood and can be characterized by displaying at least five of its nine listed criteria (American Psychiatric Association [APA], 1994, p. 661) centered on grandiosity, lack of empathy, need for attention, and entitlement:

1: Has a grandiose sense of self-importance (e.g., exaggerates achievements and talents, expects to be recognized as superior without commensurate achievements)

In the simplest terms, narcissists believe everything they complete is a massive undertaking and, according to Ashmun (2004), should be honored by all in the general vicinity. Grandiose claims are the staple of the narcissistic disorder. Frequently, the person afflicted complains that they received no assistance from co-workers or family and are exhausted by the lack of support. Ironically, often the only way to truly measure this narcissistic belief would be to visit the home or workplace to see firsthand if this were indeed the case; hence, it is difficult to actually see if the complaint is valid. In many cases, the information regarding family, friends, and co-workers is not only inaccurate, but, in reality, others may actually be taking care of the narcissist's duties as well.

A distinction between an *inflated* sense of achievement and *true* achievement is necessary in understanding the first criteria. Some individuals are boastful but truly come through with successful accomplishments. If an individual claims to be the fastest person in the world and wins the Olympic gold medal for the 100-meter run, this claim is not grandiose; it is accurate. Einstein claiming to be a mathematical genius would not have been considered grandiose by most accounts; he was. However, it is more common to meet an individual *claiming* to be extraordinary than to meet an individual who actually *is* extraordinary. Ashmun cites that most people meet "*at least* 1,000 narcissists for every genius" encountered (2004, p. 4).

2: Is preoccupied with fantasies of unlimited success, power, brilliance, beauty, or ideal love

DSM IV (APA, 1994) explains that, often, narcissistic individuals create their own realities and are disillusioned when reality invades their exaggerated sense. They may compare themselves to people of high social status or importance and complain that they have yet to be noticed and appreciated as deserved.

This characteristic may also manifest itself as excessive restlessness, lack of commitment, and frequent change in significant areas of their lives. An example may be the adult who has been through multiple marriages and claims to "outgrow" the relationships within just a few years, or even months. This person has a difficult time committing to one person for life and tends to believe there must be someone better, after tiring of the current spouse or after experiencing the reality of relationship conflicts.

3: Believes that he or she is "special" and unique and can only be understood by, or should associate with, other special or high-status people (or institutions)

The narcissist believes that others simply "do not get me" and may make the statement, "I need to be somewhere where I can be appreciated." Often, that "somewhere" is a prestigious institution or some glamorous place such as Hollywood where other successful, famous, or talented people reside. Further, DSM IV (APA, 1994) cites that to narcissists, anyone not as talented as they are appears merely average or ordinary. The narcissist scorns average and ordinary people; to the narcissistic individual, these people are worthless and do not deserve recognition.

4: Requires excessive admiration

Ashmun (2004) identifies two important aspects of this criterion. First, narcissistic, self-absorbed people crave praise continuously. They also believe whatever they do is better than what others can do or accomplish. They struggle to feel happy for others' successes, as they perceive others' rewards as attention stolen from them; thus, they often "one-up" people who share personal accomplishments. The second issue is that of *sincerity*. To the narcissist, sincerity is not a factor. The thought behind the compliment is not as important as the number of compliments given.

5: Has a sense of entitlement (i.e., unreasonable expectations of especially favorable treatment or automatic compliance with his or her expectations)

This is another strong indicator of narcissistic behavior and, unfortunately, characterizes many of today's Americans. In this regard, DSM IV (APA, 1994) explains that self-absorbed people expect everyone to adhere to their wishes, and they become frustrated if this expectation is not met. Further, the narcissist expects special treatment for all rules. They may understand the reason behind institutional rules, but feel as though their particular situations warrant exception from those rules. If they are not invited into an elite group or selected for a prestigious award, they often feel mistreated—even if they did not actually qualify for the honor.

6: Is interpersonally exploitative (i.e., takes advantage of others to achieve his or her own ends)

According to DSM IV (APA, 1994), those described by this trait use others to get whatever they want or desire. Others' thoughts, emotions, or wishes are secondary and often are not considered at all. These people are opportunists—to a fault. They may float in and out of people's lives, as they perceive that they need these people for their own advancement—personal, business, monetary, and others. The people they use may be acquaintances, friends from the past, co-workers, and even family. They are not vested emotionally in these relationships and often don't display an interest or have time to spend with others unless they feel they may get something out of it.

7: Lacks empathy; is unwilling to recognize or identify with the feelings and needs of others

The narcissist lacks compassion and is not able or willing to recognize another individual's emotions or needs, as explained in DSM IV (APA, 1994). Because of this, the narcissist typically becomes frustrated or impatient with others sharing their problems, as this takes valuable time or concern away from the narcissist. In some cases, narcissists are unable to even recognize another individual's distress and cannot understand why the person is upset. In other cases, the narcissist may see the dilemma but be unable to effectively interpret the other individual's feelings. In fact, some narcissists self-report an awareness of experiencing fewer and less intense emotions than others—but ironically perceive this as a badge of superiority over others.

8: Is often envious of others or believes that others are envious of him or her

An ever-present sense of jealousy is a common characteristic of the narcissistic individual. This sense of jealousy is often two-fold. First, narcissistic individuals are jealous of those who have material items or positions they desire. This closely parallels the sense of entitlement belief that narcissists deserve what others may possess due to their perceived unique intelligence, beauty, or talent. Second, narcissistic individuals believe others are envious of them. Thus, in their minds, admiration from others is natural and well-deserved. Further, any criticism received *must* be motivated by jealousy.

9: Shows arrogant, haughty behaviors or attitudes

Narcissists treat others as inferior. Often, the narcissists see others as "servants" and view surrounding individuals as tools to achieve their desires or goals. This quality may surface in relationships with co-workers, a spouse, or even children. Even in collaborative situations, the ideas of others are not considered respectfully, and comments may be made as to how ignorant or unrealistic others' ideas are. In extreme cases, others are treated with less-than-human measures, and the narcissists' attitudes may result in emotional or physical abuse.

As mentioned earlier, to be clinically diagnosed with NPD, a person must exhibit at least five of the nine listed criteria. By this definition, according to DSM IV (APA, 1994), less than one percent of the general population actually does have NPD. However, it is noteworthy that the publication goes on to indicate that, while many people may display the listed traits that define NPD, the disorder diagnosis is only made if the behaviors are considered "inflexible, maladaptive, and persisting and cause significant functional impairment or subjective distress" (APA, 1994, p. 661).

Additionally, even those who are diagnosed with the disorder can vary by degree. DSM IV further classifies a diagnosed client as "mild, moderate or severe" (APA, 1994, p. 2) depending on the intensity of displayed traits and the number of traits above and beyond the minimum required for diagnosis. In its most severe state, NPD can prohibit people from functioning day-to-day in ordinary social and work settings.

Obviously, the claim cannot be made that much of America is suffering from a severe, clinical form of narcissism such as NPD. However, other related conditions relevant to this disorder are currently being studied. In fact, Vaknin (2004) and others describe significant research on another form of this mental condition called acquired situational narcissism (ASN).

Robert B. Millman, a professor of psychiatry at the Weill Medical College of Cornell University, first identified this disorder, which combines elements from classic NPD and a more "transient or short-term" condition (Vaknin, 2004, p. 1). The disorder surfaces according to life's events. Specifically, ASN is a form of narcissism that develops in adolescence or adulthood and affects people as a result of wealth, fame, or other elements of being a celebrity.

In an interview conducted by Sherrill for the New York Times, Professor Millman points out that when a "billionaire or celebrity walks into the room, everyone looks at him. . . . people are drawn to this person" (2001, p. 1). A celebrity's life is *not* normal. These individuals are surrounded by an entourage of assistants, agents, photographers, lawyers, and fans at all times, which feeds the abnormal view of life. The world looks at this person so regularly and with such fascination that, eventually, the celebrated individual ceases to look back.

In many cases, Vaknin (2004) points out that ASN is merely a manifestation of earlier narcissistic traits surfacing after the onset of fame and fortune. After all, it is natural for a narcissist to seek a career connected to grandiose lifestyles, power, and fame. The identifiable behaviors become more evident as the narcissists are more frequently in the spotlight.

Unfortunately, as we often see in modern-day celebrities, the lifestyles associated with ASN are not solely glamorous. Frequently, broken marriages, drug use, legal troubles, and poor parental relationships parallel a celebrity lifestyle. In Sherrill's article (2001), Millman explains that those afflicted are incapable of seeing or understanding the reality of the world. Accordingly, rather than seeking treatment for narcissism, they are more likely to seek treatment for the symptoms that frequently accompany a narcissistic condition—depression, anxiety, and substance abuse.

Overall, a review of research shows more and more professionals are recognizing and substantiating the behaviors associated with the growing narcissism in America. Nevertheless, defining the criteria and characteristics associated with this affliction is merely the first step in truly understanding narcissism. The following additional considerations relevant to accurately identifying narcissism delineate some of its complexities.

The first major concern relates to how time and the role of societal norms influence the perceptions of narcissistic behaviors. Certain behaviors that were unheard of, or at the very least highly discouraged, in past decades have become acceptable—such as bumper-sticker bragging. Also, consider the types of birthday parties children now have compared to thirty years ago. Balloons, a group of five friends, games, and a cake would have been a major celebration at one time; now, it's not uncommon to rent laser tag facilities, inflatable play centers, and even limousines to transport the party guests.

Further, consider the explosion of cosmetic surgery in the past decade as people shop and pay for the perfect nose, breasts, or tummy (or possibly all three). Mainstream America has come to value physical beauty and perfection to the point of being willing to spend thousands of dollars and even undergo sometimes risky medical procedures to attain that perfection. Cosmetic surgery has been added to the lists of potential graduation or wedding gifts, especially for young women.

As reported in *The Week,* one plastic surgeon in Miami has written a children's book to help plastic surgery patients explain to their children why Mommy or Daddy returns home from the doctor looking not only "different . . . [but] prettier" (June 2008, p. 4). Stressing the importance of physical beauty with children and possibly connecting the notion that plastic surgery results in a new-and-improved person in some fashion would certainly have been considered vain and narcissistic by past generations.

As societal norms evolve, desires and behaviors that were once considered excessive, egotistical, and vain by many are now considered acceptable. Is it possible for society to affect the statistical growth of NPD (and the recorded occurrences of its criteria) as our perceptions of what's *excessive* change with the times? A person considered displaying "healthy narcissism" (i.e., confidence, self-assuredness, success, and pride) in today's times might have been considered "unhealthy" at an earlier time when behavioral expectations and values were different.

A second suspected complication is realizing how the nature of the narcissist could serve as a potential barrier to professional identification. For example, would someone with an inflated sense of self recognize their true qualities and seek help? Would narcissists be able to discern their lack of empathy for others and recognize it as a problem? Further, would lying and exaggeration, which have been noted as characteristic of narcissists in an attempt to bridge the gap between reality and their grandiose ideas, skew the accuracy of provided information? In other words, it would seem unlikely for narcissists to provide helpful insight in identifying their afflicting behaviors.

Also, as previously discussed, some of the criteria would seem to require extensive observation of the client in various settings of life: work, family, marriage, parenting, school, and so on. All of these factors seem limiting to making the NPD diagnosis. Overall, the general essence of the symptoms seems to limit the capability of diagnosing a personality disorder in the *owner* of the symptoms.

The third consideration in identifying narcissism relates to human development. From birth through adolescence, certain stages of development are naturally more narcissistic than others. In *Children of the Self-Absorbed,* Brown discusses "age appropriate narcissism" as a "normal part of psychological growth and development" (2001, p. 6). In a later chapter of this book we explore this idea in more detail, as it is important for educators and parents to be realistic in their expectations of a child's behavior. Incidentally, some of the most recent research notes actual differences in the physiological brain activity of people caught in these stages of narcissistic tendencies.

According to further research, critical, especially during these times, are the social and conditional factors in the developing child's life. Specifically, improper guidance or a traumatic event at a pivotal developmental stage for a child could prohibit healthy progression, whereas proper guidance and mentoring help a child mature successfully during these periods of growth.

Fogarty (2003) further illustrates the importance of proper mentoring by parents in avoiding what he terms "overindulged" children: children with inflated self-esteem, unrealistic self-concepts, a strong sense of entitlement, and the desire to control the household. His entire book focuses on the role parents often play in feeding these narcissistic qualities "under the guise of 'child-centered' parenting" (2003, p. 11). He recognizes that these parents often have good intentions; however, the end result is a country of children with more behavior problems, defiance, and detachment than ever before. In response, he offers parents insight and strategies on coaching their children out of the narcissistic periods of their youth.

As supported by research, varying degrees of narcissistic behaviors do seem to be pervasive in American culture. The United States has slowly become a more self-absorbed and "me-driven" society with alarming implications. The negative effects of these narcissistic behaviors extend well beyond the classroom, impacting many facets of life, including corporate and personal finance, family relationships, religion, and even our health and justice systems.

CHAPTER THREE

~

Societal Implications

As many social disorders are generational, vast implications exist for the issues discussed in this publication—going well beyond classroom concerns. Narcissism threatens the basic democratic ideal of working together toward similar goals and sharing aspirations for a united existence as a strong, progressive country.

In the last decade, the first implication, which involves corporate finance, has emerged with devastating results for thousands of Americans. Throughout history, many corporate scandals have taken place, and, most assuredly, America will see more in the future. Recently, though, these scandals have appeared larger—both in scale and in number. Not only have these episodes been disastrous for the company, but they have also been crippling for the thousands of Americans who have lost much or all of their life savings invested in what they perceived to be reputable, sound companies.

In what could be termed the *Enron Syndrome*, many companies now are committing drastic accounting scandals in the name of inflating profits and company positions. Many high-level employees are compensated with handsome dividends or bonuses based on company performance. As a result of this type of motivation, numerous examples of individuals in companies such as Enron, WorldCom, Tyco, and others (including high-ranking positions in government) have committed egregious, unethical acts to increase profits, hide losses, or raise stock prices. This deception has led to a declining ethical environment in the corporate world.

While dividends and bonuses seem like a logical way of rewarding corporate executives, the lines can become blurred when determining the justification for those incentives. For instance, many accounting scandals are committed in the name of showing company performance gains to lure investors to a particular organization. Increased narcissism in America could certainly be linked to this corruption. As narcissistic individuals lack the normal levels of human empathy, their decision-making is adversely affected when confronted with individual-gain versus greater-good choices. Ultimately, without thorough checks and balances, having a narcissistic individual justify his or her performance is a recipe simply asking for exaggeration or embellishment.

Corporate America is also facing another dilemma related to the topic of narcissism—how to deal with the overindulged "me generation" entering the workforce. For example, in a recent edition of *Fast Company*, Sacks (2006) discusses the new breed of worker entering corporate America. In the article, she provides examples of the chaos the newest generation of worker is causing and the enormous resources that are expended in addressing its needs. Her first illustration of the narcissistic, coddled worker is in the story of a twenty-four-year-old salesman who did not get his yearly bonus due to poor performance. Instead of the employee dealing with the problem by evaluating ways of improving productivity, his *parents* arrived at the company's regional headquarters and demanded a meeting with the CEO. Ultimately, the employee's parents were forced to leave, escorted by security.

In a second example from Sacks (2006), a twenty-two-year-old pharmaceutical employee learned he did not get a promotion. He was upset that his boss told him he needed to address his weaknesses. This criticism prompted an outraged response from his mother (yet another illustration of the "*American Idol* Reality-Check" discussed in Chapter One). The employee's mother called the human resources (HR) department seventeen times with increasingly frustrated messages and demanded a mediation session with her and her son. Amazingly, the company obliged, and at one point in the meeting, the Harvard-grad employee reprimanded the HR representative for treating his mother rudely. These young employees (and their parents) certainly show the sense of grandiosity characteristic of narcissists. Even as "twenty-somethings," they still show a warped sense of coping skills and little acceptance of adult responsibilities.

Further, while corporate finances are one issue that must be considered when addressing the topic of narcissism, the personal finances of the average American must also be considered. In a society that exalts celebrities and the celebrity lifestyles, many Americans are faced with an ever-increasing debt for consumer goods purchased in the name of improving their image and attempting to live beyond their means, as they believe they are entitled. Credit cards used to make impulse purchases to feed these narcissistic needs have paralyzed some individuals and families.

According to the Website "Filing for Bankruptcy Online," the number of bankruptcies hit an all-time high in 2005, with the majority of the cases being filed by households (versus businesses). The Website refers to a Dugas article in *USA Today* (September 15, 2003) that claims one-third of bankrupt families had credit-card debt equal to a complete year's worth of income. In general, forty percent of American households earn *less* money than they spend annually.

Unfortunately, many Americans have recently discovered the need for fiscal responsibility much too late. In addition to the bankruptcy filings, the result has been a drastic effect on the United States economy as the home foreclosure rate has reached record levels. On "World Socialist Web Site," White (2008) shares the alarming statistic released in "Tuesday by Realty-Trac" that between the years 2006 and 2007, the number of homes in some stage of foreclosure increased by seventy-five percent. Granted, not all of these foreclosures are due to overindulgence, as job loss, health care costs, interest rates, and other factors play into the equation; however, *some* are. Across the country, this trend has led to a decline in home ownership—the first decline in home prices since the 1930s Depression—and job loss for numerous employees in construction-related businesses.

Another adverse effect of widespread narcissism is the decline of the American family. As narcissists are focused mainly on their own satisfaction and pleasures, they lack the selflessness and devotion essential to being a dedicated spouse and parent. As John Rosemond (2000) consistently advocates in various publications, including *Raising a Nonviolent Child*, focusing more energy on being a family rather than fulfilling individual pleasures of family members is extremely important in developing healthy relationships. Individual needs of the parents or children should be secondary to family needs.

Too often, the narcissistic trait of "getting what *I* need out of the relationship" is the primary issue. As a result, the members of the family may in fact be pulling at the stability of the family instead of contributing to its stability and well-being. It has been widely established that a great percentage of marriages now end in divorce, and many children are growing up in "broken" homes. If the number of narcissistic individuals continues to increase, these numbers most assuredly will continue to rise.

Recently, a letter was published in the advice column "Annie's Mailbox" (December 2007) discussing the growing trend of establishing prenuptial agreements. That topic in itself is not shocking. However, one of the items addressed in recent prenuptial agreements is that some future spouses want to qualify weight gain of their partners as grounds for ending the marriage. What better example of the need to exhibit narcissistic control can be presented than a contract designed to control the appearance of the spouse of the self-absorbed?

Further, as many narcissistic individuals have a need to control much of their surroundings, marriages that do survive may not necessarily provide environments conducive to healthy, balanced child rearing. It is not an improbable stretch to continue to see increased numbers of domestic abuse charges as emotions spin out of control in the narcissistic home. Self-absorbed, "me-driven" individuals can make life difficult for a spouse or children, thereby precipitating emotional strife. As Brown (2001) explains, children of self-absorbed parents commonly respond with feelings of hopelessness, low self-esteem, problems getting along with others, feelings of isolation or alienation, and other general dissatisfaction. Logically, spouses are likely to experience similar despair.

In a recent seminar by Fogarty (2008) presenting his book on overindulgence, some statistics were provided that seem to cement the need to address the issue of living as a responsible family man. He stated that male adultery (especially for men in their twenties to thirties) is statistically increasing at an alarming rate. Fogarty suggests this is fueled by the narcissistic belief that if an individual wants to engage in this behavior, he can logically justify the need to do so. Further, adults in this same demographic are reporting an addiction to gambling at increasingly alarming rates as well. In general, instead of financially supporting their families as they should be, they are risking their livelihoods in the name of pleasure. In general, narcissistic individuals do not subscribe to the concept of boundaries, and these particular issues have great familial implications should the trends continue.

Still another aspect of overindulgence is the failure of children to learn essential coping skills to survive independently as adults. Many of today's adolescents attend regularly scheduled meetings with therapists, counselors, or psychiatrists in an effort to survive the pressures of childhood endured by so many previous generations. In addition to filling the coffers of the mental health industry, the dramatic increase in counseling ensures that children who lack coping skills are kept under the watchful eye of adults. At some point, though, this over-dependence becomes a problem.

As parodied in the 2006 movie *Failure to Launch*, a growing number of adults, especially males, are living at home with their parents. While the movie was portrayed as an entertaining comedy, it also illustrated a substantial change in the dynamics of the American family. Family physician and psychologist Leonard Sax (2006) cites a one-hundred-percent increase over the past twenty years in the number of young men (ages twenty-two to thirty-four) still living with their parents. Sax explains that the trend is happening in all demographic groups—"both rich and poor; black, white, Asian, and Hispanic; urban, suburban, and rural" (2006, p. 1). No longer are children raised to be *in*dependent, as parents excessively rush to their aid, but rather *inter*dependent. When children receive too much assistance in enduring the challenges of young life, they lack the knowledge, coping skills, and motivation to face even the typical challenges encountered in adult life.

Another example of the cultural changes currently taking place in the United States is an examination of the role of religion. According to *The Week* (October 2007), an article in *The Washington Post* (October 2007) reported that atheism is on the rise. Only six percent of those individuals in the United States over the age of sixty reported that they do not believe in God, while nearly twenty-five percent of Americans ages eighteen through twenty-two declared themselves *atheists.*

Organized religion is not immune to the implications of an ever-increasing narcissistic culture. According to psychiatric social worker Curtis Gillespie (July 21, 2008, personal communication), narcissists are incapable of loving anything or anyone unconditionally—including God or any spiritual figure. Thus, sincere devotion or piety to an organized faith among those with narcissistic tendencies is unlikely.

In addition, already, many traditions of organized religious belief have eroded, especially among the younger populations (which may or may not be considered negative depending on a person's perception of the necessity or role of the traditions in one's religious community). In fact, according to *New York Times* reporter Banerjee, "sixteen percent of American adults say they are not part of any organized faith, which makes the unaffiliated the fourth largest 'religious group'" (2008).

Traditions and customs have always served as a framework to reinforce the beliefs and "rules" of certain religions. In much the same manner that individuals in a narcissistic culture question each rule or law, the *unaffiliated* question the need for such traditions. For instance, in speaking with several twenty- to thirty-year-old individuals regarding religion, those interviewed communicated a shift in the belief of a "religion" toward a belief of "personal spirituality." In one individual's position, religion is "man-made," and spirituality is "my personal relationship" with God. This may sound like a superficial transformation to some, but in regard to the topic of this publication, it is quite critical.

This idea of the "individuality of religion" caters to the narcissistic mind-set in that it allows the individual to transform the concept of religion to a personal religion with individual rules or a customized doctrine. It disregards the community aspect of worship, the value of ceremony, and the wisdom of generational sharing. Thus the concept of religious traditions is no longer an emphasis, relieving the narcissist from the struggle of adhering to stipulations that may or may not be desirable. Remember, many narcissists desire structure or rules; they simply want the rules enforced for everyone else or altered to support their personal needs. Narcissists continue to morph individual spiritual beliefs with individual desires as justification to do what feels right.

This change from organizational religion to personal religion parallels the expectation for government, school systems, organizations, and society to perpetually incorporate new rules for individuals requesting exceptions to current policies or laws. As the number of narcissists increase, the result is a set of rules by which no one lives, drastically changing the circumstances by which we are governed. Further, if traditions or ceremonies that have taught lessons of the previous generations are discarded, some other entity inevitably steps in and fills that void. As Lasch warns, "The atrophy of older traditions of self-help has eroded everyday competence, in one area after another, and has made the individual dependent on the state, the corporation, and other bureaucracies" (1979, p. 10).

This particular implication is not meant to serve as a call for a "religious awakening" in the United States or a call to bring religion back in the public school system. That debate is better left to those leading the religious community. However, the breakdown of moral authority ultimately weakens our strength as a community of people. Whether the authority we serve is religion, a community group, our family, or our country, loyalty and service to any cause larger than ourselves is critical in uniting a society.

Additionally, just as the dogma of religion is being doubted, the doctrine of the medical profession is also being challenged by increased narcissism. It has been well documented that antibiotics are losing effectiveness due to their over-prescription by the medical community. Most medical practitioners recognize this as a problem. The question arises: If doctors know they are over-prescribing medications, why do they continue to do so at potential public peril? Quite honestly, the answer lies in the public's narcissistic refusal to take "no" for an answer.

Doctors understand that when "John" is sick and enters the office, he *expects* a prescription to fix his ailment. The last thing he will accept is the diagnosis and treatment that instructs him to eat chicken soup, drink liquids, rest, and allow nature to cure his affliction. Further, if he is given this response, he undoubtedly leaves angry and potentially seeks out different medical services. As a result, many physicians are prescribing medications they fully understand do not provide relief of the ailment, but only the mental assurance that the sickness has been addressed.

Further, expect the counseling, therapy, and pharmaceutical industries to enjoy a virtual financial windfall from the throngs of unhappy or depressed individuals needing help. Narcissistic persons frequently use a "blame-game" approach to incidents in their lives or to reactions to failures that ultimately happen to many of us. It is normal for each of us to reflect on failures in our daily lives; the critical difference is that some can accept their fault in a shortcoming, and others simply cannot. In keeping the blame somewhere other than within, narcissistic persons prefer to have a medical or psychological reason to blame. It is as if they aspire to the labels or diagnoses that frequently coincide with many of today's youth and their families. Unfortunately, educators, judges, legislators, and others have "jumped on the label bandwagon" that is so pervasive in today's educational climate.

For instance, the *New York Times* report by Carey (2007) indicates that the diagnosis for the condition known as *bipolar disease* has had a 4,000-percent increase over the years from 1994 to 2003. Many experts are beginning to examine not only the large numbers of diagnosed patients, but also the treatments used to address various psychological conditions. The purpose of this particular discussion is not to examine the validity of bipolar disorder (or other disorders) or even to determine if it is being properly diagnosed; it *is* to discuss that this alarming increase could be another "off-shoot" of a narcissistic society.

Another example of "label fascination" relates to the diagnosis of attention deficit hyperactivity disorder (ADHD). In general, much controversy surrounds the validity of this disorder. Nevertheless, whether one recognizes that ADHD is an actual affliction is irrelevant here; the more important and distressing issue is that Dr. Robert Spitzer, who was the first to identify ADHD and attention deficit disorder (ADD) several decades ago, stated in an article entitled *The Great ADHD Myth* that up to thirty percent of children diagnosed don't really have the disorder. He admits that "they may simply be showing perfectly normal signs of being happy or sad" when they are misdiagnosed (Hope, 2007).

Further, according to recent research published in *The Week* (November 2007), ADHD may be attributed to a temporary delay in brain development rather than a lifelong disorder. After researchers conducted 3-D brain scans on 446 children diagnosed with ADHD, Dr. F. Xavier Castellanos, Director of Research and Director of the Institute for Pediatric Neuroscience at New York University, explains that the brain cortex in children with ADHD was found to be underdeveloped. For most children, the cortex, which controls impulsivity and focus, develops fully by age seven-and-a-half, whereas for half the ADHD children, the cortex did not develop fully until age ten-and-a-half. Nevertheless, by about age eleven, the brain development of most ADHD children did reach "normal" expectations.

Most children diagnosed with ADHD take prescription medications to control the symptoms associated with the disorder. In examining this information, it would seem logical that if ADHD is often "outgrown" by young adolescence, the medications should also stop at that age. Unfortunately, that is not the case.

As indicated earlier, the number of school-aged children undergoing counseling is also increasing at an alarming rate. This increase has correlated with the number of students who have some sort of diagnosed mental or physical condition that must be dealt with by school personnel. Unfortunately, the success rate for these students does not appear to be increasing at the same level as the number of diagnosed students. Although this may be a controversial statement to make, for the vast majority, the therapy does not seem to provide long-term benefits.

This statement is not meant to place blame solely on therapists. Successful changes are dependent upon several factors once the student leaves the therapist's office: student and parent commitment to practice strategies and techniques designed to alter behaviors; the appropriateness of prescribed medications; and the communication between the parents, therapist, and the schools for consistent reinforcement. Without implementation of all necessary components, parents are wasting potentially both time and money. Ironically, in the future, the number of students involved in the therapy process may decline should insurance companies refuse payment for said services. This action would have been taken long ago for any *medical* procedure with a similar failure rate.

All this labeling and rush to professional treatment feeds narcissistic expectations and behaviors. As discussed earlier, narcissistic individuals have a tendency to lay blame for their faults outside of themselves. After all, if a *condition* exists that could explain their behavior and a drug could be taken to potentially control said behavior, a strong sense of relief is associated with knowing that a lack of self-discipline or control is not the cause. Further, this diagnosis may provide a sense of relief to the parent of the narcissistic child since the problem is not being attributed to poor parenting skills or the passing of genetic conditions.

A similar argument can be passed on to the judicial and justice system. Frequently, "labeled" individuals have a recognizable legal defense, and courts have been reluctant to hold children or adults accountable for behavior if they are afflicted with a condition like bipolar disorder. As a result, the normal standard of behavior that applies to every other citizen is, at times, not enforced.

Incidentally, many criminals suffer from narcissistic characteristics. Contrary to earlier accepted theories, the director of the social psychology graduate program at Florida State University, Roy Baumeister (2006), disputed that aggression in criminals and street gang members was linked to low self-esteem in his article "Violent Pride: Do People Turn Violent Because of Self-Hate, or Self-Love?" He cites evidence where "violent criminals often describe themselves as superior to others—as special, elite persons who deserve preferential treatment" (p. 3). In many cases, the criminals admitted to committing their crimes in "response to blows to self-esteem" (p. 3).

Further, Baumeister (2006) and others conducted lab studies indicating a definite correlation between narcissistic individuals and aggressive behavior toward persons who criticized their opinions. Interestingly, in their sample groups, researchers found that the "violent prisoners had a higher mean score than any other published sample" in determining the level of narcissism (p. 5).

As the culture of the United States becomes more self-absorbed, the number of criminals is likely to increase at an equal rate. A recent report in the *New York Times* (Liptak, February 2008) indicates that more than one in one-hundred American adults is currently incarcerated, and based on an article in *The Week* (March 2008), that number is higher per capita than any other industrialized nation. Narcissistic individuals have a strong sense of entitlement, justifying (in their minds) many outrageous actions. Further, narcissistic, self-absorbed behaviors are not simply found in one socioeconomic level or race. These behaviors do not discriminate. If this call to attention is not met, the need for more and larger correctional facilities will continue to be an issue for the American public.

The significant impacts of increased narcissism in America are truly disturbing. The pervasiveness of this mindset must be addressed if the previously discussed trends can be reversed. In combating narcissistic tendencies and behavior, it is important not to equate healthy self-esteem with narcissism. Incidentally, certain degrees of narcissism in certain stages of development are natural in children. Thus it is helpful to explore behaviors and other social conditions that have been found to exacerbate narcissism to an unhealthy degree. That knowledge, especially, allows parents, educators, and other professionals who work with children to become part of improving this discouraging trend.

CHAPTER FOUR

~

Stages of Child Development

A survey of the research on the topic of this publication reveals that the roots for unhealthy narcissism can be partly linked to both nurture and nature. The majority of the publications focus primarily on conditional and social factors contributing to narcissistic tendencies. The most recent research, though, draws focus to actual differences noted in the physiological brain activity between people with healthy and unhealthy narcissistic tendencies. Not surprisingly, still others connect the two, suggesting that certain factors such as parenting weaknesses or a traumatic event at a pivotal developmental stage for a child could affect the performance capabilities of specific areas of the brain. As all of these appear to play some role in fostering narcissism, it is of value to explore the stages of personality development and particularly *how and when* narcissism is most prone to develop in an individual.

The first three years of a child's life are very crucial in brain development and self-perception. Although the terminology used varies among professionals in psychological fields, basically most agree that babies are born naturally narcissistic. Hotchkiss (2002), who is a licensed clinical social worker, explains that infants are born completely focused on their own needs with the perception of the primary caregiver as an extension of themselves. Babies experience sensations such as hunger or pain *naturally,* and they cry or root *instinctually* in order to have that need fulfilled. Although from child to child these behaviors are demonstrated in varying degrees, initially no real sense of self or separation from others develops. They do expect the world to center around them—but all on an instinctual level for the first several months.

At about five or six months, babies began to explore, recognize objects, and notice distinctions in their surroundings. Hotchkiss (2002) points out, though, that the child continues to view the primary caregiver as an extension of him, and this caregiver serves as the reference in the child making sense of the new stimuli in his world. For example, Mom's fearful response to an oncoming stray dog as well as Mom's protective reaction toward her child transfers to the child's perception of the world—especially if the behaviors are repeated and patterned. It is common to see children at this age mimic a response or a facial expression of people they know.

Then around a child's first birthday, when he becomes more mobile, a sense of separation from the caregiver naturally begins. This can be a challenging period for children. They are excited about their new freedoms and abilities—but to their chagrin and sometimes confusion, their caregivers do not always share this excitement. Hotchkiss (2002) explains that when the caregiver scolds a one-year-old, the child newly experiences shame and an injured ego. This interaction between the child and caregiver is healthy and considered necessary in order for the child to begin existing more independently. It is time for the child to begin to see himself as a separate functioning individual from his parent.

Brain development during this time is very crucial. Hotchkiss cites that throughout the time of especially ten to twelve months and sixteen to eighteen months, the "part of the brain that regulates emotion is being hardwired for life" (2002, p. 40). Thus it is critical that as the child experiences this new disapproval and vulnerability, the caregiver's response enables him to also experience empathy, emotional recovery, self-control, and reassurance. The child begins to lose his delusions of grandeur and respect the caregiver as a separate being with interests, needs, and feelings independent of his own.

This process, known as *separation/individuation*, or as "learning autonomy versus shame" by developmental psychologist Erik Erikson, normally lasts until about age four. Most parents realize the ups and downs characteristic of these particular years. Many are all too familiar with grocery store temper tantrums, screaming bedtime demands, and preschool brawls for a favorite stuffed animal, especially in two- and three-year-olds. However, Erikson believes that a healthy child can "emerge from this state sure of himself, elated with his new found control, and proud rather than ashamed" (Child Development Institute [CDI]). The healthy child emerges well-equipped to progress through years four and five, as he likely spends countless hours role-playing, fantasizing, and imagining cooperatively with others his age.

Unfortunately, not all children do emerge from these years in a healthy mental state, and signs of unhealthy narcissistic qualities surface. Therapists who work with narcissists (even adults) often trace the disorder back to these critical developmental years. *Los Angeles Times* staff writer Carey explains in his article "The Narcissist, Unmasked" that brain imaging of narcissists shows activation of "areas in the brain that did not develop normally in . . . [their] second year of life"—primarily in right-brained areas affecting empathy and compassion (2002).

Carey explains that the underdevelopment could be genetic, or injury-related, but most researchers strongly propose a conditional cause. Specifically, a caregiver's reactions to the toddler's self-centered expectations are critical and can actually "freeze the boy or girl in a state of childlike grandiosity" (Carey, 2002). These are the children who continue to believe the world revolves around them, and life should be about making them happy.

In *You Owe Me! Children of Entitlement*, psychologist Namka (1997) points out examples of particular conditions that could enhance narcissistic tendencies, especially during these formative years. Children whose basic needs were not met may find themselves in a state of "ego-fixation" (Namka, 1997, p. 1) as the primary caregiver could not or did not foster the healthy development of the *self* explained earlier. Also, a child who lives with parents whose relationship is driven by one spouse consistently dominating the other may learn through observation to selfishly expect others to submit to his demands (as he has seen work in his own home).

Namka (1997) continues by citing the conditions of overindulgence. Children who are rarely denied and overly catered to do not learn healthy boundaries or self-denial. Instead, they learn gratification comes from "getting what you want when you want." In a nutshell, they learn how to *control* their home and expect to be able to similarly control other environments (playgrounds, classrooms, sports arenas, etc.).

Another condition Namka (1997) lists that may foster narcissism is when parents hold unrealistic expectations for their child, especially when the parents' egos are fed by their child's successes. For their own benefit, the parents demand the child to excel above others or risk parental disappointment and possibly even rejection. Finally, abuse and other traumatic happenings (such as divorce or death) may trigger narcissistic tendencies in children as a coping mechanism. Injured children often attempt to protect themselves from the pain, rejection, or loss experienced as a result of trauma. They want to make themselves feel important and powerful in a situation where they actually feel vulnerable and helpless.

Unfortunately, any of these conditions can have long-term effects on how the child views himself in the world and ultimately on whether he progresses through developmental stages in a healthy manner. Overall, because of the critical brain development and maturation occurring in the early years before school begins, this time is obviously paramount in determining how well a child is able to adjust in new situations—including the school setting.

Incidentally, the next stage of development identified by Erikson occurs as children are faced with adjusting to school and continues up to adolescence. Erikson refers to this stage as "industry versus inferiority" (CDI). In this stage, the child is challenged to apply the balance of self versus others learned in his small, personal world (often family) to a larger, more structured world. Environments such as school naturally impose many more rules than some children may be used to, but even more, their playing field does too.

Instead of racing a fantasy fire truck to a five-alarm blaze and then shooting off minutes later in a rocket ship to the moon, many children find themselves in dance classes or on soccer teams. Such organized activities are typically highly structured with increased playing rules. They also require a commitment to others and a sense of teamwork. Children in these years typically learn the responsibility and self-control required to be industrious, especially if they have progressed well through the earlier stages.

Social relationships change during these ages as well. According to well-known pediatrician Dr. Spock (2001), children in this age group begin to identify more with their peers than with their parents. They are especially concerned with "fitting in" to this new, large community in their lives. Unfortunately, sometimes as these friendships develop and groups are formed, certain unwritten rules about who should or should not be included into groups also evolve. Although intolerance can be common, children this age can be coached to appreciate the differences in others. They need to be provided opportunities to see the value and the necessities for various ways of living, thinking, dressing, eating, and so on. Tolerance and compassion toward others should be reinforced consistently.

With opportunities to volunteer time or to donate their allowance to the less fortunate, children this age are taught to look beyond their own needs and see the importance of serving a cause larger than themselves. Without this coaching, these school-aged children—especially those already with amplified narcissistic tendencies—continue to define "right" and "tolerable" by only what they themselves represent. In other words, these children become self-centered, close-minded, and self-serving.

The final stage of development before adulthood is the teenage years. As most would guess, these years (much like the first three or four years) are critically formative. Interestingly, Hotchkiss (2002) compares teenage years to the ten- to twelve-month and sixteen- to eighteen-month periods where long-term, unhealthy narcissism is more likely to develop than any other time. As explained earlier, this is especially true if the teens' basic needs are not appropriately met and they do not emerge with a balanced view of themselves.

Physiologically, according to renowned author and speaker Dr. Riera (2003), a teenager's brain again undergoes extensive growth, especially in the areas that control rational thinking and decision making. In Riera's words, "teenagers' impulses are way ahead of their abilities to control them" (2003, p. 23). Similarly, *LiveScience* staff writer Goudarzi (2006) cites a study that suggests a teenager's brain may be incapable of processing compassion, empathy, and guilt as adults would. This study also attributes this distinction to differences in the maturity of certain areas of the brain. Thus teenage thinking (at least for a while) is commonly stuck in a natural stage of narcissistic behavior. This type of thinking causes many teens to act impulsively to satisfy themselves with little regard as to how these actions affect others. Further, when questioned, they may struggle to explain or justify their behaviors.

Many teens also experience immense self-consciousness in their struggle to discover their identity. Ironically, as teens are spending a great deal of energy tapping into their individuality and uniqueness, they are also preoccupied with blending in to a certain idealization created by their peers and even the media. They become hyper-aware of blemishes, clothing trends, name-brand anything, hairstyles, body types, cosmetic colors, handbags, and so on. This preoccupation can manifest itself in harmful narcissistic behaviors if a teen also makes overindulgent demands and feels entitled to have all the latest and greatest (even more so if the caregiver submits to these demands).

Another characteristic of a teenager's life that leads to natural narcissism is the increased opportunity to be center stage. As previously mentioned, technology has fueled the situational narcissist's fire. In today's culture, adolescents are not limited to being physically *visible* in their individual towns; they can be visible anywhere in the world. Websites allowing photo or video postings feed the belief that these individuals are more talented and more attention-worthy than they may truly be. Again, blaming the Internet and social Websites such as YouTube, Facebook, and MySpace for all narcissism in our society would be simplistic and naïve, but these Websites do play a role in the *degree* of narcissism and self-absorbed behavior people exhibit, in much the same manner as a casino is responsible for a gambling addiction. The Internet is merely the vehicle through which the narcissists can feed their need for attention.

Even before the latest means of technology with Websites such as YouTube, teenagers were establishing stardom in their high school gymnasiums, band rooms, and performing arts centers. For most of us, no other period in our lives provides so many opportunities to join groups or teams that show-case and award individual talents. In one year, a student could realistically be captain of the volleyball team, cheerleader, Homecoming queen, play cast member, starting softball pitcher, and valedictorian of her class. This amount of attention does *not* take place with the average adult!

Don't be mistaken—experiences such as these are important and quite valuable to an adolescent's maturity. Many teens through the years could be poster children for excelling *due to* the limelight. Performing in front of others develops several positive traits including confidence, discipline, and poise—as well as humility *if handled well*. These qualities constitute healthy narcissism and equip the teen with valuable adult skills.

As explained in the "Stages of Social-Emotional Development in Children and Teenagers" provided by the Child Development Institute, Erikson finds that a healthy adolescence results in a self-confident, achieving, constructive individual. He cites that it is common for teens to experiment in various roles and seek positive role models for inspiration. Of course, some of these experiments prove to be more beneficial than others; eventually, though, many teens establish a unique identity with solid values.

Understanding the physiological brain development in children that may create states of natural narcissism is valuable, but without question, it is even more valuable to recognize the behaviors of others and social conditions that exacerbate natural narcissism to an unhealthy degree in some persons. The individuals who do not evolve beyond healthy narcissism are the focus of our concern, as these people—both students and adults alike—are creating challenges in education that are both frustrating and detrimental.

~

CHAPTER FIVE

Narcissistic Parents
in the School Setting

As outlined in the stages of child development, all individuals experience a time in human development when a "me focus" is natural, healthy, and, indeed, necessary. Nevertheless, this time should pass—well before the stages of parenting begin. Healthy, self-actualized adults realize that they and their loved ones have faults of their own and understand their role in assuming a healthy mental frame of mind. The concern is that more and more Americans are not fully evolving from this "me-centered" stage and are having difficulty adapting later in life. Educators are seeing the fallout of this phenomenon as they deal with increasing numbers of narcissistic parents with each passing year.

Often the school setting can appear to be a private club or "society" of which some parents love to become a part—similar to the Hollywood scene, but on a *much* smaller scale. As discussed in Chapter Two, the concept of acquired situational narcissism (ASN) theorizes that a situation can take place that prompts previously suppressed narcissistic traits to emerge. "Situations" take place daily in the school setting that could serve as the springboard for these characteristics to surface. If daily situations can exacerbate narcissistic traits, then common individuals should realize they too can get "caught up" in self-absorbed behaviors. Overall, many situations can occur that bring about a "big fish in a small pond" fame for the parents of school children and, as a result, elicit narcissistic traits.

For example, for the parent of a student who is a star athlete, frequent attention can surface at every turn, especially in small towns or suburbs. Merely going to the grocery can be an affirmation of one's status in town, as friends and neighbors compliment on-the-field successes. Often, these compliments are directed to the parent as well as the student: "You must be so proud" or "He played a great game last night." Additionally, newspapers and local television stations frequently feature stories on athletes and the attention garnered by colleges and universities. Even major networks such as ESPN are now covering and televising the high school games of highly touted recruits. Narcissistic people believe they are on stage, and for these individuals, they are—twenty or thirty times in a basketball season, for example.

This "fame" is bound to have an impact on the mental psyche of the students as well as their parents. Narcissism in athletics makes the coaching process very difficult. Many coaches lament that today's parents would rather their child get the individual title of "All-State" as opposed to the team making it to a state tournament. Further, parents increasingly question coaches' decisions on team selection and playing time, particularly their own child's, of course. This narcissistic desire for attention and sense of entitlement leads to demands contrary to what is best for the team.

A similar mindset takes place in virtually every facet of the school environment; athletics is simply one area of the school setting affected. The same "fame" can be thrust upon the talented musician, star of the play, valedictorian, or gifted artist. The "fan base" for any of these students can get "caught up in the moment" as well and demand the *just due* for that particular group or individual. In true narcissistic situations, the students of various groups and their parents often become engaged in a battle of justification for greater attention during this time. This whirlwind can be a virtual nightmare for school personnel who must balance equal treatment, media coverage, visibility at events, and equally distributed compliments to all involved in an effort to avoid favoring one aspect of the school.

Other situations that sometimes foster narcissistic traits in parents involve volunteerism. As strange as that may sound, some parents' motivation for volunteering at school centers on attaining privileges for their children and themselves. For example, often large-scale trips, such as an annual Washington, D.C., pilgrimage, need a fund-raiser chairperson or a chaperone coordinator. As some volunteers become more involved in their positions and their presence in the school becomes more regular, their persona changes as well. Volunteers may enjoy the status that comes with calling community members "on behalf of the school," and these individuals may even have occasion to run events that put them *in charge* of school personnel. These people begin to see themselves as important—in some cases, as a supervisor of staff and students.

These parents' volunteerism can come with a price tag to the school when they expect preferential treatment or leniency of rules. Suppose for a moment that an individual arrives early at a school event (unrelated to the volunteer assignment), and the doors are scheduled to open at 7:00 p.m. Outrage can ensue if this individual is treated as everyone else. The thought process tends to be, "Doesn't the person monitoring the door realize who I am—I work here!"

Many educators realize that narcissistic parents have an adverse effect on school children. Often narcissistic parents are overbearing and *too* engaged in their children's education. We have heard some of these parents described as "helicopter parents" because they are always "hovering" over their children, involved in every activity, and assisting to extreme measures. Sadly, though these parents may have good intentions, often the self-absorbed child's mental growth and development is retarded in many ways.

For example, many of today's young children lack coping skills. The perpetual cycle of protection, victimization, and immaturity present in children who grow and live with the helicopter parent threatens healthy development. Consider the following example of overbearing, narcissistic parents and their daughter, Sally:

> Sally is in grade school and is experiencing difficulty with a fellow classmate. The parents discuss the day's events with their daughter, and Sally indicates that this student has called her a name and "made fun" of the clothes she wore to school. As loving, protective parents, they tell Sally that they will call the school, and if this student causes her distress again tomorrow, to let them know immediately. Of course, they follow through and call the teacher the next morning.

Sally's parents' reaction is a typical happening in many of today's schools and classrooms. The best-intentioned parents are dealing with all sorts of childhood dilemmas in the name of "bullying prevention" and "self-esteem building." Unfortunately, the illustration described here can lead to negative consequences later when the child is faced with handling situations on her own accord.

Using the same illustration, consider for a moment what Sally does not learn. She does not learn what to say in this situation, who to approach at school for assistance, and how to proceed if the situation worsens. Through her parents' haste to solve her dilemma, she is not armed with conflict resolution skills necessary for her developmental growth.

In addition to discussing what Sally did not learn, it is equally important to examine the unspoken messages that Sally may have gleaned from her parents' reaction. She is simply taught the unspoken message that she is a fragile and delicate child incapable of taking care of herself. This particular message—especially when repeated again and again—has lasting consequences for children. They should feel empowered to handle adversity appropriately, which is best learned through experience.

Incidentally, conflict resolution skills are taught in many elementary and middle schools across the country today. However, if one were to investigate, much of this instruction did not occur as recently as fifteen to twenty years ago. What has changed? We believe that much of this instruction is needed because children have not been allowed (because of overprotective caretakers) to address situations that arise in daily life.

Additionally, as both a school psychologist and family counselor, Fogarty (2003) has studied self-absorbed behaviors for years and points to a strong correlation between child conduct disorders and self-absorbed parenting techniques. Despite the common stereotype of "spoiled, rich kids," Fogarty stresses that overindulged children are not solely the product of wealthy families. Although some children who are fortunate to come from homes with good financial situations are, in fact, self-absorbed, simply having wealth is not the precursor for such behavior. As indicated earlier in this publication, studies show that overindulgence is not simply a class or culture issue. However, distinct differences may exist in how the overindulgence of parents is typically manifested among various groups.

Fogarty (2003) shares the example of a young male who was having difficulty finding a parking spot in the morning before school. As this student lived in a wealthy community, instead of requiring that the student get up earlier to "beat the rush" or ride the bus, his parents simply purchased the home across the street from the school so he would be guaranteed to always have a parking spot. Further, his parents gave him the keys to the home so he would have a quiet place to study after school. These parents have prevented this young man from learning to solve a minor problem and accepting responsibility. Instead, his minor inconvenience turned into an excuse for being showered with luxury. This style of problem solving encourages this young man to be lazy and demanding.

Children in lower class, poorer families can be raised in a narcissistic setting as well. Rather than providing too many material goods, these parents tend to provide too many privileges. Sadly, many educators have sat through meetings with a parent and a child where the child perpetually interrupts, corrects, or demeans the parent. Essentially, the child is ruling the household. As an educator, it is frustrating to watch a child tell a parent, "That's not how it happened; you are so stupid. Let me tell the story." Even when school personnel step in to correct the child in this setting and curb the disrespect, moments when the parent still rushes in and defends the child's behavior unfortunately still occur.

Another concern Fogarty (2003) correlates with children being raised in an overindulgent environment is that children often develop *inflated* self-esteems. They are rarely required to face disappointment or humility (which are realities in life). When quick-fixes and approval are constantly provided, a paradox is created: Children are perpetually given the message they are entitled and superior, but they do not have the discretion to discern between appropriate and inappropriate behaviors in common life situations. In the school setting, these children struggle to accept criticism or challenge from authority. Often, their reaction in such situations is to respond disrespectfully. Then, if the parents are brought into the situation, a vicious cycle ensues, as they characteristically support the child.

With sometimes the best of intentions, narcissistic parents cite reasons such as child protection, unconditional love, high expectations, or even school support as their justification for excessive interference. Several characteristics are now becoming the "norm" as the trend to demand individual attention and treatment has increased. The following is a sample list of those traits or mindsets common to parents who exhibit narcissism. Although this particular list was not generated based on scientific research, testing, or extensive data gathering, many readers working in the K–12 public education arena will likely be able to visualize individual parents who exhibit these traits in their current situations.

Personality Characteristics of Narcissistic Parents

1. Believe their child deserves all that is good in life and deserves the best of all rewards; they demand their child be placed in certain classes with certain teachers, even if the child has not met qualifying requirements for a class; they have an exaggerated sense of the child's abilities or capabilities, as they believe their child's accomplishments reflect on *their* abilities; the narcissistic parent thrives on positive feedback.

2. Believe it is their duty to control day-to-day happenings in a child's school day; they are overly involved in school activities of their children, desiring constant communication so they can address any deficiencies; they depend excessively on technology or other means for knowing their child's homework and grades.

3. Believe that school personnel are servants to their child's (or their) needs and education; they feel the school must be willing to address

their family needs or crises without exception, and their needs to be addressed are frequent.

4. Believe that rules are vital for the school to be successful and structure is important; however, their needs or crises are sufficient grounds to supersede those rules; special treatment is often requested.

5. Believe that problems are personal attacks on them or their parenting skills; thus, they take ownership of their child's problem and feel it is their responsibility to fix the problem.

6. Believe they can "fix" issues and just need to be kept informed of all their child's activities—almost as if they (the parents) are on the school staff; they frequently attempt to discuss other students with the staff as well in relation to their child's problems.

7. Believe their child learns *in spite of* staff rather than *with* the assistance of staff or due to staff efforts; they may even claim their child's successes are solely due to their efforts as a parent rather than the work of school personnel.

8. Believe their child qualifies (or should have qualified) for any and all special recognitions, rewards, services, or incentives issued by the school or district; this may also include "labels" that are issued to special education students; they see their child struggling to get good grades and hastily want to discuss accommodations the school can make, rather than the child's lack of effort.

9. Believe issues of the child (or even the child him or herself) are "burdens" on them and any issues are now a "cross to bear" when parenting is necessary; they are sometimes difficult to reach as they often do not respond to phone calls regarding their child; if appointments are agreed upon, the parent often cancels at the last minute.

10. Believe their child is more responsible than those of his or her peer group; they act in disbelief when negative statements are made regarding behavior; sometimes, these parents have the "We Never See That" response to negative school calls or deny that their child is capable of the related infraction.

11. Believe that their child always follows through—even when they do not; if an error has been made, they assume it is usually due to a mistake on the part of the school personnel; for example, if a parent were to require the child show a daily log of assignments and the child failed to do so, the parent would assume the school staff would be to blame, as they did not send one home: "If the school is not going to be consistent, there is no sense in me or my child following through."

Again, this list is not all-inclusive, and many other items could potentially be added when describing the mindset of the "me culture" becoming more pervasive with each year.

Not surprisingly, school personnel forced to address these parents often feel mentally and physically drained after discussing educational issues with them. In an effort to control all that is near and dear, the narcissistic parent manipulates, berates, badgers, or pressures others to fulfill their wants and desires under the premise of "loving and doing what is best for my child." Actually, after having dealt with the parents over the years, we've recognized a growing popularity with certain styles of reaction or debate.

In a major cultural shift, parents have a "rush to action" mentality when their children face conflict. Historically, parents would listen to the child complain about the school, teachers, other students, or coaches, and then provide advice in dealing with those individuals. Often, children need to "vent" and the parent can represent the sounding board necessary for this "blowing off steam" moment for the child. However, many of today's parents—in a controlling, protective stance—listen to each complaint and feel a strong desire to be sympathetic and supportive. This support usually manifests itself in a "call to action" where the parent telephones the school official and makes demands. As the population of parents using this approach increases, the stress and strain on the school personnel can be overwhelming.

Generations ago, parents believed that enduring tough times built "scar tissue," and struggling was not necessarily viewed as a bad thing. In fact, the adage "that which does not kill me makes me stronger" was professed as appropriate childhood encouragement. That philosophy fosters the development of perseverance, empathy, compassion, and sympathy for others experiencing some plight of their own. A movement to eliminate this aspect of the maturation process appears to exist. Often, parents protect children with a justification of remembering "what it was like when I was a child and my child will not go through those times." Lost in this theory is the ability to recognize how enduring challenges precipitate healthy maturation into adulthood. On the contrary, protecting children from conflict and disappointment sets them up for painful awakenings in future years.

When school children have the beliefs illustrated here and those beliefs are perpetually reinforced and defended at home, the child lacks the basic coping skills necessary to handle *any* adversity, let alone items as traumatic as getting dumped by a boyfriend or girlfriend, bullying by a peer, or bad grades. These items are particularly upsetting to a pupil in grades seven through twelve. Then, when parents sense the lack of coping skills necessary to handle such adversity, their reaction is to "rush to the aid of the loving child." This repeated rush-to-aid reaction further exacerbates the problem by providing another example of how the child's issues are at the forefront of the minds of the many adults that surround him or her each day. A vicious cycle ensues.

It is plausible to make the argument that children *should* go through tough times and these tough moments are not always negative. If a child has gone through adolescence unscathed, this is not only a very negative sign; it is an indication of a child unable to adequately handle the trials and tribulations of adult life. This "protectionist" point of view is provided by the justification that "today's children are exposed to so much more than ever before." While this may be true, exposure alone does not assist a child. If this were the case, exposing a child to the washing machine would teach them how to do the laundry. Only practical skills *taught* and the opportunity to *use* those skills truly *prepare* a child.

A second common reaction is the "blame it on a condition" phenomenon. Most educators recognize that the most common reason for students failing courses in school is the student's failure to complete homework. Homework provides practice for learning class material for future tests, and in many cases, provides opportunity for teachers to record more easily attained points between tests. Unfortunately, some parents do not seem to follow that reasoning. Even after being told their child is not completing assignments, narcissistic parents insist on identifying a condition to explain away the poor grades—test anxiety, low self-esteem, concentration problems, and so on.

Instead of placing the responsibility of the failing grades on the child, they push to find a cause beyond their or their child's control. An increasing number of parents are requesting their children be evaluated for learning disabilities, even after a team of educators determines no suspicion of such a problem. In many of these cases, improvements in work ethic and study habits are the magic cure they are seeking. Unfortunately, the time and money spent throughout the process to reach this common-sense solution is extensive, and these resources could be used much more effectively on those who really need it.

In a third common argument, which can be termed as the "Clinton justification," the narcissistic individual focuses on every word in a discussion of an issue rather than the message itself. The words are scrutinized to such an extent that the original issue becomes lost during the conversation. This type of evasive argument was characteristic of Bill Clinton, who was the presidential candidate who "tried marijuana, but did not inhale." A further example concerning Mr. Clinton occurred during the "Monica Lewinsky scandal" in the late 1990s. When questioned in a television interview about his involvement with the young intern, President Clinton looked directly into the camera and claimed to the American people, "I did not have sexual relations with that woman." However, in time, proof of his intimacy with Ms. Lewinsky surfaced. Had President Clinton lied to America? Ironically, the answer to that question was not as obvious as it first appeared, as the debate that ensued across the country was about the *definition* of "sexual relations."

Prior to this scandal, most Americans would have considered fellatio (the alleged action) to be a sexual act. However, throughout the next few months, these same people began to seriously debate whether this (oral sex) was actually "sex." Incidentally, a long-term repercussion of this debate is the increase in the number of teenage girls who consider themselves "virgins" if they only engage in oral sex with their partners. Nonetheless, throughout those months of debate, the most important issue in the Clinton/Lewinsky scandal should have been whether or not the president divulged the truth, but it was not. His alleged deceit was overshadowed by the classification of the sexual act in question.

To fully blame President Clinton for argument based on semantics would be unfair and unintentional. Further, this particular example is not made to exhort a particular political point of view or make judgments on the Clinton presidency. Many presidents and politicians have lied, told half-truths, or altered policy for their personal benefit. However, President Clinton very successfully "connected" with the American people at a time when narcissistic behaviors and poor parenting were increasing. As a result, the occurrences of reasoning by semantics appear to have increased after this episode in U.S. history.

Educators encounter this style of argument frequently, as illustrated by the following discipline scenario:

> Johnny is accused of spray-painting his name on the side of the school one Monday evening. The administration calls him to the office to discuss the issue. The principal mistakenly asks Johnny if he committed this offense Tuesday night after he left the building. Johnny replies that he did not. Later, the principal is able to provide witnesses who observed Johnny committing the act, and Johnny is suspended—both for vandalizing and for lying to the administration.

The reaction of narcissistic, self-absorbed parents and students is easily predicted. Johnny states, "You asked me if I did it on *Tuesday;* the vandalism was done on *Monday.* Therefore, I did not lie, and the suspension for lying should be reduced." Also, Johnny's parents argue that, "If you are not even certain enough of the details as to know *when* the vandalism occurred, we do not know how you can be so sure *who* did it. He deserves no punishment at all." Immediately, the discussion is now focused on the administration and the inaccurate detail in questioning as opposed to the student, the vandalism, and the unethical act of lying when questioned by authority.

Another style of argument common with the narcissistic parent is the "at least he didn't kill anybody" justification. Typically, this argument piggybacks a school employee's complaints about a child's behavior. The child may be disrupting the educational process by repeatedly getting out of his seat, talking, refusing to cooperate with the teacher, failing to do assignments, and picking on other students. Nevertheless, the educator must be prepared to respond to parents when they state, "These sound like typical adolescent behaviors; what is the big deal? It is not like he punched someone, brought a weapon to school, or *tried to kill anybody!*" The parent attempts to minimize the problem by comparing the behavior that was committed to that of one that was not.

If prepared, educators can "steal the thunder" of the parent and beat them to this argument. A successful strategy is to begin the meeting by stating, "I am glad you came in, as we need to discuss your son's behavior. He has been acting up, and we need to get his attention. The behaviors at this point are not severe, but they are getting in the way of his (and others') learning. We did not call you here to suggest you take him out of school; after all, it is *not like he tried to kill anybody,* but we must address what he is doing—as the smaller behaviors are adding up."

Once the meeting facilitators have used this logic and made the parents' argument their own, the parent has little recourse other than to agree. At that moment, the meeting can proceed in a positive manner and the real issues can be discussed. After all, repeated small discipline issues over time can be more frustrating than a single major incident.

In all of these scenarios discussed and the defense methods displayed by parents, the primary (and critical) ingredient missing is the support for the school. Not too many decades ago, school personnel and parents were viewed as being on the same team. Frankly, in many cases, when a student received punishment at school, follow-up punishment at home was a guarantee (and often more feared). Times have changed.

Those who study education and enter its ranks are usually familiar with the phrase *in loco parentis*. Loosely translated, this Latin phrase means "in the absence of the parent" and was meant to provide a framework for caring for children in the school system. Today, in some cases, this phrase could more appropriately be changed to mean, "in replacement of the parent" or even "in spite of the parent." Many parents develop a continual adversarial and mistrusting relationship with the school. In a growing narcissistic culture, this relationship only continues to deteriorate.

CHAPTER SIX

~

Narcissistic Students in the School Setting

For educators, narcissistic parents pose just one round of the "battle" in the ring. Parents' punches and knockdown attitudes toward school and educators often do not remain unnoticed by their children. Between mimicking others and falling for the "you deserve it all for nothing" messages in our society, students have become increasingly narcissistic as well.

As a nation, we are failing children in America as they struggle to progress through the "Me Stage" of development into a more realistic view of self and society at large. When a child is first beginning to show signs of overindulgent, narcissistic tendencies, the worst approach is to continue to foster those tendencies. However, some parents, caretakers, and even teachers excessively fear that any criticism or failure demoralizes or devalues a child. As a result, some adults have gone overboard to create the opposite effect.

Even the school environment can at times encourage student narcissism as well. For instance, over the years schools have adopted programs for honoring students that ultimately do more harm than good. Recognizing students for *true* accomplishments is important and serves as a good motivator for some. Recognition can also help to build a person's self-esteem as a result of experiencing success and accomplishment.

Unfortunately, many of these recognition ceremonies have lost this sense of purpose and have become travesties. In many schools—especially for younger children—school personnel strategically plan such events so that every student receives at least one honor. Educators are even sometimes inventing awards or handing out "last place" ribbons (of course without calling them that) just so every student can be honored. How is it an honor to be recognized when every other person in the class is also being recognized?

Using a similar philosophy, several schools or individual educators have also eliminated activities or practices that could potentially rank or place one student above another in the educational setting. As an example, consider one elementary teacher's method for selecting a "Student of the Month," a program in which all teachers in the school are asked to participate. Most teachers select students who earn good grades, show improvement, excel on a particular project, work hard, and so on. However, one teacher opts to select her honored student another way. She decides that the students should nominate themselves for Student of the Month by submitting their name with a reason they deserve this honor. Each month, the teacher then blindly selects one of these names from a box, and that student is named the honored student.

This teacher took a program designed to reward educational achievement and hard work (thereby helping to build self-esteem) and warped it to avoid excluding any student. Unfortunately, instead of encouraging positive behaviors from students, the program actually does the reverse. First, if the students are determining whether they deserve to be honored or not, who will be the first to drop their card in the box? Of course, those who seek attention and feel entitled to that special treatment (keystones of narcissism) nominate themselves. In effect, that teacher is inviting students to display narcissistic qualities. Humility is completely discouraged in this process, as students have no chance to be selected unless they nominate themselves. Further, the contest, in reality, has become a lottery or competition of luck rather than recognition of achievement.

Imagine the mixed messages to other students when the child who receives perpetual discipline, does poorly in class, and interrupts the educational process for other children is now honored as "Student of the Month" and is pictured in the local newspaper as a child of distinction. Further, imagine explaining to the child's parents how issues at school may need to be addressed when he was just recently honored as arguably the "best" student in the class. What about students in this teacher's classroom who do meet the traditional criteria established for the program? They quite possibly do not receive the recognition they do deserve. Overall, in an attempt to protect those who may not excel in school, the misused program now has ill effects.

Building self-esteem is important in developing children, but true self-esteem is directly connected to achievement, effort, and success. Those qualities must precede praise in order to reinforce a healthy self-concept. For the Student-of-the-Month example, at the very least, the staff member should have discussions with each student and review the "self-referrals" to determine if they are accurate. Asking a student to reflect on their behavior, work-ethic, or ability can be good, but allowing false and exaggerated impressions of one's abilities and traits is neither healthy nor positive for a child's development.

Thus, students should be guided to recognize their strengths *and* their weaknesses as they mature. Self-actualization is very important in becoming a healthy adult. In a nutshell, ideally, people recognize their strengths and perpetually develop and use these strengths to excel—*and* to overcome what they recognize as their weaknesses. It is perfectly healthy to realize one's own limitations, and recognizing one's faults should not be considered a "blow" to one's self-esteem.

When children are showered with undeserved praise and are not held accountable for negative actions, the foundation for future confusion begins to take shape. The mere concept of positive reinforcement or praise begins to "lose its luster" if the child has received literally hundreds of compliments previously—especially if the compliment is given for the sole purpose of complimenting.

On a large scale, competition in the educational setting has seemingly taken on a negative connotation. Remember the previously discussed elimination of red ink when scoring student papers and the demise of naming valedictorians and salutatorians by the high school in Boulder. Rather than allowing students to learn the positive traits associated with losing, the new belief is that all students can receive the positive effects of perpetually winning.

In reality, students who do not finish first in competition can walk away with several lessons:

- First, next time "I" need to do *this one thing* if I want to win the competition; that one thing could be practice harder, study longer, or use a different approach; any such reflection is positive for an individual to learn.
- Second, children learn the value of humility and grace if faced with a situation where they know they did their best and still finished second (or even worse); no one can be the best at everything; children need to understand this as well and not believe they are *entitled* to first prize in everything they do.
- Last, children learn the value of not giving up when things do not ultimately end with desired outcomes; many children simply quit if an activity is challenging, trying, or negative in any way.

Positive lessons can be learned from failure, but these lessons are quickly being eroded and replaced by a "fair and just" movement where all students are winners and all students receive equal accolades. Imagine some of our greatest inventors and the results of their work if they had been satisfactorily praised and lauded for what did *not* work or if they had given up their work as a result of experiencing failure.

As school children become more narcissistic, they also begin to demonstrate the negative characteristics and personality traits associated with this personality disorder. One of the most severe forms is in people's lack of ability to see themselves as contributing members to the rest of society. As a result of this "loss of perception," one tragic impact on the American student could be the rash of shootings that have taken place in many schools and universities across the country. The October 12, 2007, episode of the popular television show *Dr. Phil* analyzed these shootings and the involved gunmen. According to the show, as of that date 323 children had been killed in school shootings since 1996 in seventy-three total events. Dr. Phil McGraw's guest on this particular show included Dr. David Buss, a professor of psychology and author of *The Murderer Next Door*, and Ms. Pat Brown, a criminal profiler.

As shared by Dr. Buss, most shooters shared anger or frustration due to some form of public humiliation during the time frame leading up to the shooting. This humiliation was often reported to be in the form of getting "dumped" by a girlfriend, being bullied or "pranked" by a classmate, or feeling persecuted by some school personnel. These events can and do occur. Naturally, they also generate hurt, angry, and even desperate feelings. We certainly do not condone bullying or harassment, but even more strongly, we cannot condone such a violent reaction to those events.

As the guests pointed out on the show, many students have been enduring all of these behaviors and feelings for decades without reacting with such hatred and rage. What has changed in recent history? How have these young people come to justify such extreme reactions? As the experts on this show identified personality traits of the typical school shooter, startling commonalities to narcissistic personality traits were revealed.

According to Brown, one of the personality traits common in school shooters is the sense of entitlement. These students believed they were justified in what they did. In several cases, details of the shootings were planned well in advance, and in some cases, to a very disturbing degree. Ms. Brown stresses that school shooters "do not just snap"; rather, they are teens that, due to several factors in their lives, are "disaffected." It is not uncommon for shooters to have a mental health history or legal history.

These disturbed teens may have learned to defend misbehavior with "victim justification" at a very early age. They may rationalize their actions by citing they were victims of bullying and nobody at school did anything about it. Indeed, messages have been shared that the shooters felt the victims deserved whatever they got because "I've been hurt"—rather than taking the "high road" and rationally dealing with their hurt. These young people did deserve peace in their lives, but certainly not at the expense of others' lives.

Second, school shooters profiled often made grandiose moves to ensure they would be remembered. Typically with media involvement, these strategies worked. Through social networking sites, the Internet is often used to leave postings outlining the plans and justifications for the killing. In addition, many students typically tell others about their plans. According to Mc-Graw (2007), seventy-five percent of school shooters do tell someone before the crime happens. Some experts characterize this as a "call for help" when the argument could just as easily be made to characterize these actions and statements as a "call for attention." Further, several school shooters have left notes or videotapes expressing satisfaction that as a result of their crime they would be remembered and known, even if it is posthumously. Despite the carnage created, the attention they expect to receive seems gratifying.

Finally, the featured school shooters often possessed a "me against the world" view of society. In many regards, narcissists view their lives as independent from the rest of society, often holding society in contempt—*especially* when a member of society would dare challenge their opinions, skills, intelligence, or appearance. Many school shooters have been identified (by themselves or others) as loners or misfits. This is an important point in this discussion, as narcissistic individuals often fail to see themselves as part of society. Thus, they have less difficulty striking out against something to which they feel they do not belong.

Characteristics such as a sense of entitlement, grandiosity, and social disconnectedness are at the foundation of a narcissistic personality disorder (NPD). Is every school shooter a person afflicted with NPD? Probably not, and this is not the purpose of this publication, as the observations of two experienced educators are not proper training to make such a diagnosis. However, the commonalities in the profiles of a school shooter and the narcissist—alongside the increase of both groups in our society—do not seem completely coincidental.

This rise in teen violence is not just in relation to school shootings; teen-on-teen violence has also increased in relation to Internet postings. In a disturbing trend, some teens have been misleadingly luring others to private locations for the sole purpose of committing violent attacks to be videotaped and uploaded to social and video Websites.

Sadly, many of these attacks have left victims both mentally and physically disabled—sometimes permanently. Nevertheless, the instigators of these assaults somehow experience some emotional high by posting these events for others to view. In holding with narcissistic characteristics, the teens misconstrue the number of visitor "hits" as "fans" of their actions. In some cases, as other teens see the visits to these sites, efforts are made to *outdo* the previous postings and ensure their place in the fame associated with committing such heinous acts.

Another much less dramatic effect of narcissism on school children is cheating in schools. Cheating is on the rise at an alarming rate in schools and universities across the United States. In fact, according to ABC News journalist James (2008), Donald McCabe of Clemson University surveyed 24,000 students in seventy educational institutions and learned that sixty-four percent of all students are involved in either sharing completed work with others or using cheat notes. He cites that the level of cheating has never been so high and very little remorse is connected to cheating.

Furthermore, also according to James (2008), parents were often involved; twenty-five percent of the students surveyed revealed their parents had completed over half of at least one school assignment for them. In another survey administered by Rutgers Management Education Center in New Jersey, ninety percent of all high school students admit to homework cheating with nearly sixty-seven percent admitting to more serious cheating. Clearly, when ninety percent of all high school students are cheating, this situation has reached epidemic proportions!

When students are confronted with such behaviors, their reactions are disheartening. Two themes typically emerge. First, in the "Bill Clinton" justification style, many students attempt to evade the crime by stating, "It depends on your definition of cheating!" Again, the focus is not on plagiarism, copying another's answers, or academic dishonesty; rather, the semantics of the "crime" are examined. Again, narcissistic, self-absorbed persons rarely accept responsibility for shortcomings. Instead, they place blame on other issues or divert attention to another discussion.

Parents often use this approach as well. We have conducted meetings with parents regarding plagiarism and even had one parent exclaim, "I know he did not cheat on his paper because I wrote it for him!" Imagine the dilemma in trying to get the parent to understand that cheating is taking credit for someone's work that is not your own, even if it is someone in the family.

The second cheating theme to emerge was the "bottom-line" approach to academic work. The bottom-line approach rationalizes that the work was completed on time and the answers were correct. Students are proud of the fact that goals were met, good grades may have been received, and positive reinforcement potentially came from parents and staff. The manner in which that took place becomes secondary to the importance of the time and productivity factors. This is similar to the "Enron Syndrome," discussed previously, in which any means necessary to an end are valued as long as the company makes money—the bottom line is met.

A third effect of narcissism on students is the decline of true altruism. As that statement challenges the general character of our young population, it is important to again recognize that not all young people are narcissistic. In fact, statistics show that volunteerism itself is high among teenagers, and the media frequently provides coverage of young people involved in Habitat for Humanity or church-related mission trips. In other words, altruistic, people-serving adolescents do exist in our society.

Having said that, though, we have experienced an equally growing trend of students seeking attention or reward for volunteerism. Over the years, many non-profit organizations and school programs have attached motivations, incentives, and even mandates to charity projects or community service. For instance, in order to collect items in the food-drive campaign for the needy, students are offered a pizza party as reward for donating their cans of green beans or asparagus. Also, many schools across the nation impose a community service mandate as a requirement for earning a high school diploma. The theory behind encouraging young people to serve at a local soup kitchen is good, but when such a task is done only because it is required, the true meaning of service is lost.

Further examples of serving for payback are rampant in the media. Recently, a young man found a class ring that belonged to an alumnus of a neighboring school district. Instead of simply contacting that school and returning the ring, the parent of this young man first made plans to contact the media so his kindness could be locally showcased. On a more global scale, celebrities may volunteer their services in areas of underprivileged countries. They may donate large sums of money and interact closely with suffering—but for some, not without an entourage of media to broadcast their efforts to their fans.

Incentives and recognition are being attached more and more to serving others. Unfortunately, more rewards exist to motivate, and more students are being rewarded for little. This trend perpetuates the narcissistic idea of doing something for others only when some personal reward is gained. Many might argue, "But if good deeds are done, who cares what the motivation is? After all, no one is really hurt if the people running the charity keep eighty percent of the money for themselves; twenty percent still goes to charity and *some* people are better off!" This point has some validity—but even more irony. If we are to make strides in reversing the "me-driven" craze so prevalent today, then sincerity in our efforts must be addressed. There must be a point in every situation where personal validation ends and sincerity begins.

The point needs to be made that American students are indeed *capable* of altruistic initiatives (and often more willing than many adults). Many students simply need the coinciding educational value of such endeavors if behavior is to be shaped and formed. But if students are not exposed to altruistic concepts, given the necessary coping skills for adversity, and allowed to practice those skills, the narcissistic, self-absorbed, consumer-driven culture in which we indulge may expand and the costs continue to rise.

Overall, the effects of narcissism are leading to a steady decline in morality and an erosion in the general respect for other human beings. In correlation, throughout our many years in education, we have witnessed the following personality traits emerging in a growing number of school children. Again, experienced educators will undoubtedly visualize present and past students as they peruse the list.

Personality Characteristics of Narcissistic Students

1. Believe their level of education is based primarily on the work of others; may make statements, "I did not learn a thing in that class; if I had a better teacher, I would have been better prepared."
2. Believe their work is often better than it really is; these students have a higher sense of self-worth in regard to projects or individual answers on tests or assignments (especially assignments or projects when grading is more subjective in nature).
3. Believe their effort put forth is greater than that of their peers—even if it is the same in relation to actual time spent; for instance, they may make the statement, "I worked on it for two hours, too, but it is harder for me because I have to try harder."
4. Believe it is most important to spend a great deal of time in school cultivating social relationships or connecting with extracurricular activities that garner attention for individual accomplishments.
5. Believe they could be as good as anyone else who excels, and dismiss others' accomplishments by making such claims as, "I could get better grades, but I don't want to be a nerd" or "I could be an athlete

if I wanted to spend all my time in the weight room and do nothing else"; these students distinctly differ from those who may make some of these same statements as defense mechanisms to avoid feelings of inferiority, in that they truly believe they could and blatantly dismiss others' achievements and talents.

6. Believe their "issue" is a crisis for the school and may often make the statement that "someone should do something about this!"

7. Believe in conflict resolution, but this process can only begin when others agree with their perspective.

8. Believe that other students are "out to get them," and others are jealous of their looks, abilities, or intelligence.

9. Believe they are under more pressure because so many others "look up to them and admire them" and are jealous of what they can do or what they have; also, believe the admiration is justified and they have a sense of entitlement for these same reasons.

10. Believe that the school needs rules, but their circumstances dictate a justification for leniency when those rules should be applied; they make the statement, "I can't believe I got punished for this. I never do anything wrong. I'm the good kid."

11. Believe they fit the criteria for every incentive, reward, or accolade offered and may be offended if not chosen for such rewards.

It is no surprise to see many students exhibiting these traits. If one were to examine both listings provided in this publication for narcissistic parents and students, a pattern of behavior soon materializes. Narcissistic, self-absorbed students bemoan some treatment by school personnel, and narcissistic, self-absorbed parents demand a meeting to address their concerns and justification for special leniency. Over and over, these young people are told, shown, and taught that narcissistic attitudes and behaviors are the means for "getting what you want."

As a result, like the narcissistic parents, a growing number of students exhibit several common narcissistic reactions when they are faced with situations that may test their patience or character. Students also argue semantics (the "Clinton" justification), blame their weaknesses on factors beyond their control, and minimize their crime by pointing out that "at least they didn't kill anybody." Additional common arguments surface as well.

For instance, one common conversation point with many students defending an action is the "you forced me to" argument. For example, when students miss school for reasons not excused by the school handbook, often they report being sick or having medical appointments in order to avoid negative school consequences. In their minds, they have reasoned that their absence was justified and that the school is wrong. Thus, it becomes easy for them to also then lie about the reason for being absent. If the truth is discovered and the student is confronted, a common response is "you (the school) forced me to lie; if I had told the truth, I would have been punished." Rather than focus on the need to attend school and possibly endure some uncomfortable moments, the need to be dishonest is somehow justified in the eyes of narcissists, especially if the dishonesty results in their fulfilling their personal needs or desires.

Students often cite this same argument when they have been involved in cheating. As previously discussed, cheating is reaching epidemic proportions, and many students do not seem to view cheating with much remorse. While the *act* of cheating itself is not a hallmark characteristic of narcissism, the reactions or justifications for many of these students may be narcissistic in nature. Often when students are caught, they blame the "pressures" placed on them by society, their parents, or the school.

In their minds, these pressures force them to cheat to get by. Certain universities are harder to get into, so they cheat to meet the requirements. Parents expect honor roll, so they cheat to get the grades. All their teachers gave homework or scheduled tests for the same day, so they cheat to reduce the work. Rarely do we hear that students cheat because the work is truly too difficult (of course, that is still not okay). They are usually looking to take the easy way out to get a good grade.

A second common reaction of narcissistic-natured students is the "I deserve respect, no matter what" mindset. These students themselves may not be showing respect as they more often display the ability, freedom, and audacity to attack authority when their stance on an issue is questioned. Nevertheless, they expect to be shown respect. Such students tend to treat authority figures as being on equal ground (at best). They *demand* respect and often attempt to dictate policy, second-guess assessment, or debate every detail with school personnel. Most educators have learned to not engage in power struggles with students, but these students crave the last word and spar tirelessly until that goal has been achieved.

Parenting expert John Rosemond often points to the child-rearing techniques of today's parents as much of the culprit for many of these behaviors. In his book *Parent Power* (1990), he outlines the decline of respect for authority when children believe they are on equal footing with adults. When small children are routinely reasoned with and provided complicated rationales for parent decisions, a child matures believing they are entitled to a reason or justification for virtually every rule that may prevent them from getting what they want. Seldom do children hear the phrase "because I said so," and many young parents vow to never use this reply with their children.

Unfortunately, school teachers with twenty to thirty elementary students do not find themselves with adequate time to explain the reason behind every classroom rule and then debate the necessity for such a rule. Sometimes individuals under the direction of an authority figure need to accept conditions out of sheer respect. The diminishing respect of the adult/child or teacher/student relationship only fosters the inflated sense of self so many students exhibit today.

In addition to the decline of respect for professionals, a decline in the respect for social etiquette is apparent. It is not uncommon for today's student to divulge personal bits of information that would have been sacred and private until recent years. For example, it would not be unheard of for a female student to burst into an administrator's office where two educators are having a professional conversation and exclaim, "I can't believe he is telling everyone we finally had sex! Can you believe he would tell all his friends and ruin my reputation?" In this example, the student did not exhibit the basic etiquette of not interrupting, but then went further by exploding with quite personal information in the presence of school personnel.

This boldness is common with many of today's students. Students heavily focused on "self" are quite free with private details, as they fail to distinguish between their world and their surroundings. They assume everyone would want to be drawn in to their concerns and are not cognizant of the need to filter information based on who is listening. Again, consider how many young people are posting private information on social Websites for *all* to read and not thinking for a moment about the significance of sharing such personal information.

A final common reaction in narcissistic students is to focus on the end. Many educators see an overall erosion in the *desire* for knowledge and true learning. While most parents, students, and school personnel cite the need for education to be successful in a fast-paced and technical world, many students approach coursework as a *checklist* to be completed for their desired outcomes. Those outcomes usually consist of college transcripts, resumes, diploma requirements, grade point averages, or class rankings. For many, gone are the days when students mention the need to learn the material for the knowledge or expertise to excel in a profession or to lay the educational foundation for future coursework. Further exemplifying the approach the narcissist uses toward education, virtually all aspects of education, classes, and scholarships are merely viewed as the vehicle to "get what I want."

All across the country, an increasing number of college students are enrolled in remediation courses. One commonly cited explanation for this trend is the lack of preparation in high school. Often it is difficult to get students to take more difficult coursework due to the added workload associated with those courses.

When students are solicited for advanced courses, the next common strategy of action is the "sales job" required to get students to accept the challenge of the class. Often the student states, "What is the benefit of taking this class? It's not what I want to major in." Or "I want to take an easier class to help increase my GPA my senior year." Or, referring again to an argument discussed earlier in this chapter, "I am under pressure to get the best grades, and I need the easiest classes possible." Fortunately, colleges do seem to be evaluating senior-year coursework more than they used to in determining acceptance. Even then, taking a course to be accepted into a college falls short of taking a course to learn.

The purpose of this chapter is not to unabatedly bash American school children. In fact, many of these issues point out that students are not necessarily to *blame;* they are simply the product of the culture in which we live, the parenting they receive, and the education "experts" provide. In much the same illustration that it is impossible to take back words that have already been spoken and often very difficult to undo damage rendered, it may be equally challenging to "undo" the mistakes of the past in parenting styles and educational movements. If widespread efforts are not embraced, in many respects, a generation of students may be lost to these mistakes, and society bears the consequences, not only for this "lost generation" but possibly also for their children.

CHAPTER SEVEN

~

Education's Role
in the Growth of Narcissism

In examining the growth of narcissistic tendencies in a greater societal context, it is also necessary to evaluate some of the causes for how we have reached this point in America's history. Specifically, as we have focused primarily on narcissism and its relationship to education in this publication, we would be remiss to not reflect on public education's role in the problem. Have school programs fed into the self-absorbed "Me" movement? Have educators fostered or encouraged children to hang on to the selfish, narcissistic traits that traditionally accompany toddlerhood and adolescence? To answer these questions, it is important to review some of the highlights in the history of education and the movements that spawned today's philosophies and beliefs in regard to the growth and education of the American child.

For centuries America was commonly referred to as "the melting pot." Our country was viewed as the golden nugget of opportunity, and millions traded their livelihoods, families, homes, and sometimes their lives trying to "become an American." The driving belief was that if one could just safely get to America—no matter where he arrived from—he could learn to "fit in" and live the American dream. From clothing to language to career opportunities, people craved assimilation into the American lifestyle.

However, in recent decades, rather than America being referred to as the melting pot, more commonly our country has been referred to as a "tossed salad." The mixing of multiple backgrounds continues, but the pressure or desire to assimilate has lessened. The country is better represented as a mixture of individuals living together with a goal of harmony and the added "flavor" of mixed ingredients of differing cultural backgrounds and beliefs. The differences remain intact, still within one population—thus, the "tossed salad" identification.

Throughout its history, the world of education in America has experienced a similar change in philosophy. In the early years, educational programs were definitely designed as "one size fits all" where the goals and curriculum were very specific. All students were expected to learn what was taught, how it was taught. Obviously, over time, this level of conformity has evolved greatly and schools have also become "tossed salads." Serving individual differences has, without question, become the theme of American education.

Much like the good that comes with respecting ethnic and cultural differences, numerous benefits also exist with respecting individual learner's needs and differences. Every good teacher realizes the importance of continually evaluating learners' strengths and weaknesses and adapting instruction to reach optimal success. However, as time passes, we see the benefits of such differentiation reaching a breaking point. Our concern is that as the world is becoming more and more diverse—not in skin color or religious beliefs, but in values, priorities, and ways of thinking—the list of individual needs and differences is growing to unattainable proportions.

Politicians' platforms and media headlines across the country are quick to point out that the public education system is broken—basically in the same manner and for the same reasons that government is, at times, ineffective. The focus for both has become far too varied with too many special interest groups. As our society becomes more narcissistic, people call on the government and education alike to attempt to be all things to all people. Most rational people realize the impracticality of this lofty goal. At some point, if public education is to progress effectively, it becomes necessary to establish rules, standards, or guidelines that foster a "bigger than me" mentality in the learner and that do not attempt to respond to every request or proposal.

In *Common Sense: A New Conversation about Public Education*, Kelley (2003) describes the simplicity of the first schools in the United States in the 1630s where education was established to directly reflect the Puritan lifestyle and beliefs. Even as the student body expanded over this century from the original elite groups of scholars- and ministers-in-training to eventually include all white children, the focus of instruction remained consistent: learning to read and write to better understand Scripture.

The first challenge to this curriculum occurred over a century later. Kelley (2003) explains that some of the conservative leaders of the time sought a program that would teach young people more discipline. Actually one conservative went so far as to point out the ill effects too much knowledge may have on one's morality. These conservative leaders stressed the need to com-bine a religion-based education with an additional focus on "self-sacrifice, patriotism, and loyalty" (2003, p. 6). Granted, the changes were subtle in nature and probably altered the educational landscape very little; neverthe-less, for the first time in American history, state leaders were instrumental in determining the direction of public education.

One of the first major historical movements to influence the progression of public education was the Industrial Revolution—with both intense and widespread changes. Industrialization spurned new challenges in American cities, and, according to Kelley, educational leaders determinedly looked to the school system to be the "great equalizer" for a country in a state of chaotic advancement (2003, p. 10).

The next question facing the newly industrialized society, though, was what to teach in these schools. Rapidly, the backgrounds of the students were becoming more diversified. The skills needed for employment were more complex because of many new inventions and society's industrial-ization. Further, the social challenges of students were greater than ever because of the widespread poor living conditions. Already in these early years, we see that as the world becomes more complicated, public education certainly does too.

These schools by the end of the nineteenth century and early twentieth century were certainly beginning to take on the look of today's modern education. As cited by Kelley (2003), by 1918, all students in all states were mandated to attend school; school boards were setting the mandate for teacher training, school design, and curriculum; and perhaps most impor-tantly, the role of schools was expanding as it was being directly influenced by social and economical developments of the times.

In the next decades, the American people saw exploding advancements in technology. Kelley (2003) explains that throughout the conflicts and pressures of World War I, the Depression, and World War II, the United States increased educational spending on science, research, and engineering in order to get an edge in both the military and non-military marketplaces. Through these times, the interest in education and competition with other countries were high. Most people strongly believed in the industry-focused school system that had emerged in the United States.

However, one educational movement beginning around the 1920s, initiated primarily by John Dewey, challenged the current system. As Kel-ley (2003) describes, Dewey pushed for a "child-centered education" in a movement that eventually became known as the "Theory of Progressive Education." His theory emphasized that learning should not focus on sheer concrete facts, but should integrate those facts practically and fully into developing a complete individual capable of thriving in a complex society.

Although Dewey's ideas received widespread attention—even beyond America—the concept never seemed to gain enough momentum to overshadow the technological and scientific focus still imminent in the United States. Quite possibly, though, his ideas, followed by various others throughout these decades, spawned the notion that schools were failing individual learners. It is possible the longstanding debate of whether educators should see their primary role as teaching children or teaching a subject matter has its roots in the movement initiated by John Dewey.

The 1950s were typically characterized as a decade of optimism in the United States, though public education was not without controversy. According to Bracey (2007), some of the publications most critical of schools, including Rudolf Flesch's *Why Johnny Can't Read*, were written at that time. Then on October 4, 1957, the Russians launched Sputnik I into space, which, as explained by Kelley, became the event with the most "profound and pervasive effect that a single . . . event has had on this country, particularly in regards to education" (2003, p. 17).

Sputnik caused a panicked response in America in a desperate attempt not to lose the position of being the most powerful nation in the world. A distraught United States struggled to understand how such an event could have taken place, and as Bracey (2007) explains, among several possible explanations, the most popular theory to surface was that Russia had better schools. Whether that theory was accurate or not, reactions to address this problem were predominately aimed at education. Under the leadership of President John F. Kennedy, the United States vowed to not fall behind any other country (particularly Russia) in space exploration.

As a result, according to Kelley, a huge campaign was launched to motivate young Americans to become part of the grand effort to "not only save America but also to save the world" (2003, p. 18). The students' calling or primary role in the campaign was to attend college—even though at the time fewer than eighteen percent of the students in schools were on track to do that, and less than half were even graduating. Young people were persuaded that a college degree equated with money and future success, and that "it was one's patriotic duty to go on to college and become a professional—preferably a scientist or engineer" (2003, p. 18). A rippling shift from vocational education to college-prep curriculum soon took place in public education, and the educational practice of ability grouping began as an attempt to identify, separate, and adequately prepare those who fit that newly defined mold for success early.

Not surprisingly, teachers also experienced some effects from the rapid changes in education as they experienced more public criticism and public pressure to meet new demands. Many educators sensed the need to protect themselves as professionals, and teachers' unions began forming. Thus began the often-pervasive struggle between union demands versus administration (at all levels). Incidentally, as the leaders of our country pushed for schools to produce engineers and scientists specifically, Kelley (2003) explains that the leaders of the National Education Association advocated a much less aggressive program in which students were trained to *think*. As a result, the differing goals created tensions in regard to day-to-day operations in the school.

As the 1960s progressed, schools continued to directly feel the events of the times. The turbulent years surrounding the John F. Kennedy assassination, various civil rights movements, desegregation, and the Vietnam War changed school operations. As Kelley explains, "the nation was polarizing" on several issues that "bewildered and confused" many, especially the adolescents and young adults who feared these challenges "would destroy them and their generation" (2003, p. 24). Specifically, the heavily emotional Vietnam War involvement zapped the patriotism of many.

At the same time, statistics show a significant decline in church attendance and religious interest among families, as illustrated by Kelley (2003). People were struggling to find a uniting force in the nation—whether it be patriotism, faith, leadership, or something else. Then, in the early 1970s, Madeline Murray O'Hair initiated the debate that led the movement to ban religion from public schools. Ironically, the very ideals that public schools were built on were being taken out of the system.

Students—and parents—had lost faith in the leadership and establishments that once brought them security and promise. Unfortunately, this included the institution of public education. Not long after the push to make education top priority and for all to become college graduates, America saw droves of students dropping out of high school and choosing nontraditional lifestyles with little responsibility and structure, often with little regard for ethics or law.

Faced with much more than academic curriculum concerns, schools brought on various programs to address the anger and bewilderment of the young people. For instance, Lyons (1995) credits a 1966 publication by Lawrence Kohlberg with bringing character education into the schools during this time. Although many supported the need for this type of instruction, differences of opinion existed on how it should be implemented. Some feared that teachers would impose their personal values on students rather than students realizing their own values. Individuality and "doing what feels right" was certainly surfacing as a popular theme in the country.

The other program that stormed the nation around the same time was the self-esteem movement. This movement may have had the most dramatic implications in regard to the narcissistic, self-absorbed effects we are faced with today. Bronson points out that in 1969 Nathaniel Branden published *The Psychology of Self-Esteem,* which advocated that one's "self-esteem was the single most important facet of a person" (2007, p. 3).

Also, according to Rosemond (2006), in 1971, Dorothy Briggs published a best-selling book called *Your Child's Self-Esteem* that encouraged parents to give children equal voices in household decision making. Rosemond explains that Briggs strongly advocated that if children were to survive in a democratic society, they should be nurtured in a democratic family; further, children should *have* what they *want.* As a result of these (and other) publications, self-esteem education became the newest buzz phrase in public schools. Incidentally, since 1970, over 15,000 scholarly publications have been written on the values of self-esteem education alone.

Both character education and self-esteem education were taken on by schools at all levels and thus began the controversy, which still exists today. Do these programs work together or against one another? For some, character education and self-esteem development worked hand-in-hand with the theory that a higher self-concept contributed to being a better person and better student. For others, the two programs clashed as some experts felt self-esteem education created unmotivated, self-centered individuals who needed proper character development. To confuse an already muddled discussion, other controversial programs such as sex and drug education were designed and assigned to schools to address students' social lifestyles.

Another important focus in education that saw pivotal changes in the late 1960s and 1970s was equalization for females and the disabled. In addition to guaranteeing certain opportunities for each of these groups, Super (2005) explains that the Education for All Handicapped Children Act of 1975 mandated individualized educational programs (IEPs) for all disabled children. As has been pointed out with other educational changes, in meeting these mandates, several approaches and theories have come and gone over the years.

For instance, the use of resource rooms to isolate IEP students from other students took place for years in an attempt to meet their individual needs. Then, the proverbial pendulum began to swing, and the push for placing IEP students in the least restricted environment (LRE) became the favored approach. As the years have passed, more and more IEP students have been "included" in the traditional classrooms with modifications and accommodations in an attempt to successfully assimilate them into mainstream society.

The 1970s' focus of serving the disabled students sparked attention to the individual learning needs of gifted and talented students as well. By the next decade, federal legislation—the Jacob K. Javits Gifted and Talented Students Education Act—was enforced, as explained on the U.S. Department of Education Website at www.ed.gov. The actual implementation of the act could be determined by the individual states, but eventually the majority of the states mandated customizing gifted students' education. With these programs, too, however, controversy still exists as to whether educators can best serve these students' needs by pulling them out of traditional classrooms or by implementing differentiated instruction within their individual classes.

As Super (2005) describes, one hot educational approach of the 1970s attempted to address individual needs of all students—open education. For high school students, open education often meant fewer required courses and more electives. Educational programs were primarily driven by students' interests, and the instruction was centered on active, media-focused lessons. But again the pendulum swung, and by the end of the 1970s this program was blamed for decreasing school achievement and lower standardized test scores. Ironically, many of the schools constructed during the era of open education were designed with fewer walls and large, spacious areas to support this style of education. Not long after, when the program failed, these same districts scrambled to add temporary walls and create a more self-contained classroom environment.

Since that time, this revolving door of proposing new education theories, adding state and federal legislation, adopting new instructional programs, and throwing out programs has become a way of life in education. Educators at all levels, politicians, parents, and students seem to recognize that the system is broken, and each constituent has suggestions how to fix it. The end result has been an exhausting amount of time, money, and energy spent on implementing all of the supposed solutions.

One current movement being touted by some politicians and educational leaders is the push for a national curriculum. Some see this solution as the equalizer for public schools across America, as they envision uniform core course instruction or even a streamlined morals and values educational program. Others strongly oppose the idea. David Ferrero (2005), the director of Education Research and Evaluation at the Bill and Melinda Gates Foundation, points out that those who desire such a curriculum would probably not like the ultimate product should such an endeavor come to fruition. As a national curriculum could only be derived through great compromise (or complete dictatorship), few would be truly satisfied with the "agreed upon" plan in the end.

Imposing such extreme uniformity on a diverse American population is too simplistic. Likewise, overindulging or catering to the needs of *every* child is not healthy either. Ultimately, regardless of the curriculum and its level of diversity, a child should be encouraged to take control of his or her learning and realize the consequences for not doing so. This premise should garner little debate and much agreement—sadly it does not.

The historical and continual shift to focus on the individual learner and address his or her specific needs on all levels of student ability from the lowest special education student to the most talented and gifted student has ultimately, in many cases, taken control of learning away from the learner and placed the greatest pressure on and required the greatest efforts from the staff and school. Ironically, many of the most significant educational movements took place during or after the presidential era of John F. Kennedy, who made famous the phrase, "Ask not what your country can do for you; ask what you can do for your country." In educational terms, the students (and parents) *are* apparently asking what the school can do for them.

These most recent generational parenting and schooling techniques have enabled children to be placed on a pedestal and made to feel as though their desires, self-esteem, and feelings are paramount to all with whom they work. Excessively addressing individual needs in some respects has fueled the narcissism explosion as well. School personnel are often met with laundry lists of personal needs to address and issues to resolve. Unfortunately, responding to these laundry lists—especially of narcissistic individuals—often results in an even longer laundry list. Schools must regain a level of obligation where consistent effectiveness can realistically be attained.

CHAPTER EIGHT

~

Strategies for Examining and Reducing Narcissism in Schools

The display of narcissistic traits in the school setting must be addressed. If not, school personnel increasingly become "servants" to every individual need and issue for every child. While *legitimate* issues for individuals are *truly* important, it is important that legitimate issues do not simply or automatically translate into a dependency on institutions or another task for the overburdened personnel who may work in those institutions.

The education of a child can only be *truly* effective if all parties—school personnel, the parents, and the child—are active participants. Further, the involvement of each must be productive. The parent or child *demanding* attention to their concerns is *not* an example of active participation. Rather, it is an example of the sense of entitlement pervasive in many school children and their families today.

It is easy to be pessimistic and simply state why the system is "broken" and that the world is doomed for failure. The difficulty lies in stating what steps can be taken to address the problems described. Offering solutions frequently opens the door for skepticism or criticism; however, searching for ways to better handle the effects of increasing narcissistic behaviors in our society is our driving force for this publication.

Thus, the following pages of this chapter contain suggestions, which could be used by schools or districts to address these issues and alleviate the practices that lead to the exacerbation of a narcissistic culture or self-absorbed families:

1. The school personnel should avoid taking the common conflicts, battles, and demands of a person with narcissistic tendencies to heart. Just as a

therapist would tell a spouse of a narcissistic individual to avoid internalizing some demands or criticisms of the relationship, school staff members should do the same and be ever mindful of their role in the educational process. At all costs, the staff should avoid allowing issues with this type of individual to become personal. Educators should focus their efforts in teaching, lesson plans, and student achievement and not allow the "vampire-like" tendencies of the narcissistic student or parent to "suck the life" out of a career.

The best advice is to avoid the power struggles, debates, and arguments associated with working with these individuals. While explaining procedure, policy, and protocol is always the best approach with constituents, students and parents with narcissistic tendencies often merely use the explanation as a further contention for debate. For example, if a student is being punished for carrying a cell phone, the parents may ask, "What is the purpose for the rule?" If school personnel indicate that one reason for not allowing cell phones during the school day is to circumvent cheating, the parent may immediately state, "But that is not what he was doing, so he should not be accused of something he was not doing." At the point in the discussion when the *policy* is called into question, overindulgent parents may ask for an "exception."

When policy is questioned after it has been explained, it is best to simply redirect the discussion. School staff should proceed with statements such as, "I'm sorry, but it is the policy of the district to address students with cell phones. I have done that, and we will just have to disagree on this issue." As explained by psychiatric social worker C. Gillespie (July 21, 2008, personal communication), a heated discussion only feeds a narcissist's mindset. If the educator becomes angry and "acts out," that educator has simply validated the narcissist's negative opinion of that individual as a professional, and the narcissist continues to believe he is right.

Further discussions and conversations on this topic often are fruitless and tiresome. As a result, we recommend that the conversation remain civil and professional, but it should change directions. Rather than allowing a debate to ensue as to the value of the school policy, the discussion should address future actions and how the involved student can proceed successfully.

2. Educators should reflect on the aspects of narcissism they themselves possess and evaluate how those qualities influence their job performance. As a citizen of American culture, school personnel are bound to possess at least a small amount of these self-absorbed tendencies. In the most commercialized society in the world, inevitably teachers are going to be faced with some aspect of this issue individually. If American society is becoming increasingly narcissistic and the culture of the generation of students leaving the universities is more "me-driven," then it is reasonable to assume the behavior of school personnel

is dramatically changing as well. After all, the population of future teachers is taken from the very me-generation culture entering the professional ranks.

It is easy for educators to complain (and often they do) about the excessive demands placed on their daily list of duties to accomplish. This publication was not meant to inspire support for "the downtrodden educator" who claims to be overworked and underpaid. Nor was it meant to serve as justification for doing less in educational efforts. The very nature of education should be altruistic, and in that vein, serving others is just part of the job description. However, some educators, in some moments or situations, forget they do not work in isolation and fail to see how their actions affect the larger school setting. Remember, when addressing any school issue, the concerns of all parties should focus most heavily on the education, learning, and achievement of the student.

Due to this fact, the following list was established so school personnel can reflect on their dealings with students, parents, colleagues, and the administration. After reviewing this list, educators are encouraged to revisit their behaviors and address deficiencies that can ultimately hurt the school as an organization.

Personality Characteristics of Narcissistic Educators

1. Believe in teacher accountability for others but let themselves "off the hook" with poor student performance under the premise of "Look what I started with" or "Of course those teachers did better—they have better students."
2. Believe the administration should not let others "get by" with unprofessional behavior or poor performance, but feel attacked should those same standards be applied to them or their work or behavior.
3. Believe successes in their teaching are a result of their efforts alone, and credit should be given for those efforts; statements may be made similar to the following: "Yes, the school had success, but after I did this activity all year, look how well *my* students performed."
4. Believe they have struggled to get to this point in their career and frequently remind other colleagues, students, and administrators of this fact; these claims may or may not be true, but they are a major issue in the minds of these individuals.
5. Believe they are the "master of their domain" and are offended at the mere thought of being questioned for the reason behind a project or the suggestion for another approach to teaching.
6. Believe their personal issues are extremely important and discuss them at great length with other personnel or administration; their

personal "issues" or "crises" are also regular occurrences throughout the school year.

7. Believe their needs are of greater importance than those of their colleagues; for example, if field trips are curtailed, they agree this cutback should take place, but complain that "My trip is such an educational endeavor, though," or supplies should be limited due to budget cuts, but "I *must* have mine to teach adequately."

8. Believe there are "reasons" or excuses for their failures that are bound to take place—there are always external reasons for failure to obtain goals. Further, these individuals fail to accept constructive criticism, even in small degrees. An example may be the employee who is outraged at being evaluated as merely *satisfactory*, when he clearly believes he should have been categorized as *exceptional* or *outstanding*.

9. Believe their opinions are vital to all discussions—may monopolize staff or departmental meetings by pushing their agendas.

10. Believe they teach in a "one-room school house" and fail to realize the consequences for the group when decisions are made in regard to issues such as student discipline, grading, or curriculum; they may make statements such as, "It is better to ask for forgiveness than permission—just do it and apologize later."

Before school personnel become defensive and begin to justify many of the behaviors listed, it is important to note that these behaviors affect all individuals in a society so afflicted by narcissistic traits. Since we as educators are not immune, it is wise to examine the degree of personal implication and the effect of our behaviors and mindsets on the school setting.

Further, just as the general population dictates the personality of the future teacher, the population of teachers typically indicates the personality of the future administration. Administrators do have a bearing on the school setting, and the tone of the building is often set by the personality of the individual in charge. As narcissistic, self-absorbed individuals typically value prestige and control, it is entirely possible to have a narcissistic individual leading the building or district. As a result, the following list was created in an effort for administration to reflect as well, thus leaving no stone unturned in the school environment.

Personality Characteristics of the Narcissistic Administrators

1. Believe that school improvements take place due to their efforts alone and staff must be "forced" to assist in the process.

2. Believe students, staff, parents, and higher administration are obstacles in school initiatives; if others would simply listen to and do what they desire, things would be easier and the world would be a better place.

3. Believe that personal issues or crises are important and frequently discuss those issues with colleagues and support staff; these discussions can be particularly harmful at the administrative level because others may feel inhibited about limiting certain topics with a superior and feel uncomfortable; not only is the discussion counterproductive to work productivity, but it is also potentially detrimental to professional relationships.

4. Believe that "external forces" are too overwhelming for progress to be made; the building or district cannot get better due to things such as socioeconomic level of students, poor central office, poor teachers' union officials, and so on.

5. Believe the issues of their buildings are the most important for the district and should be resolved immediately.

6. Believe their research on issues is the most relevant and disregard the research of other administrators and staff when addressing school issues.

7. Believe their decisions regarding issues such as discipline are absolute and should not be questioned.

8. Believe that their "career" is the most important aspect of their chosen profession; they may perpetually look for other positions of higher esteem, income, or prestige.

9. Believe the intention of professional dialogue is to promote their own agenda or philosophy rather than entertain others' thoughts or ideas; would not be characterized as a good listener by students, staff, or parents; may "hear" what others have to say, but do not truly listen to others' opinions or ideas.

10. Believe the achievements of others may be a "threat" to their leadership or reputation; they may be fearful of not being looked upon as the "expert" in an area under their control.

Fair or not, educators are often held to higher standards in the public's eye. Our attitudes and behaviors are scrutinized; thus, it is critical that educators possess a realistic view of themselves as to where they fall on the problem/solution scale.

3. The next suggestion is important, especially when working with older students. When school personnel have meetings with today's parent regarding learning or behavior, they should place as much responsibility on the

child as he or she can assume. It should not be considered a "successful" meeting if at the conclusion, a "grocery list" of tasks for the staff members is created with no duties specified for the parent and, more importantly, the child. Being able to demand responsibilities from the staff merely feeds the feeling of power or control of the parent or student.

For those with narcissistic tendencies, control is paramount to their personality. Therefore, it is increasingly necessary to give the parents tasks for progress, and to give the student tasks that the parent is responsible for overseeing. The teacher and school need to share responsibility, but leaving with all tasks assigned to school personnel only feeds narcissistic behavior. The worst thing that can take place is to assume *all* the responsibility and to feed the ever-hungry monster that is the narcissistic parent or student.

For example, if the student is doing poorly in class and a meeting is scheduled to address those difficulties, common strategies or interventions are often used to address those concerns. Often school personnel are left with some (or all) of the following tasks:

- Call each time a homework assignment is not complete.
- Change teaching strategies or assignments to accommodate the child.
- Phone the night before a test or quiz is administered.
- Phone or e-mail if the student is off-task or not paying attention in class.

All of these strategies may sound reasonable, but if one were to examine where the efforts fall, it is readily apparent that the staff members have accepted all responsibility for improvement. Without parental support or student "buy-in," no improvement is recognized. Research has supported the need for parent and student involvement for greater student achievement. Merely requesting information does not qualify as true involvement. Parents and students should be expected to address deficiencies in a collegial manner with school personnel.

In addition, educators must document ideas generated in these meetings specifically and copiously! Narcissistic students and parents often alter, twist, and change the outcomes of meetings or conversations for their purposes. Taking quality, detailed notes can be a vital step in combating this particular issue. Documentation items could include the following:

- Date and time of meeting
- Method of meeting or conversation (phone, face-to-face meeting, written letter, etc.)

- Topics of discussion
- Tasks to be completed
- Persons responsible for tasks
- Date of follow-up meeting (if necessary)

Overall, narcissistic attitudes have resulted in less student and parent owner-ship of education. Keeping them responsible and accountable, as educators are expected to be, could be key in changing this mindset.

4. Closely related to the previous suggestion is a solution that could po-tentially require some change of thought and practice by many educators. Parents with narcissistic tendencies may attempt to exhibit control by want-ing to "be in the know" at all times. This control usually translates into staff chasing students down to sign homework slips and agenda books or providing an outline every day of assignments to be completed. These records allow the parent to track all student progress so the parent can "prevent" academic difficulties before they happen. These extra duties may not be an issue if the staff member has one or two students for whom they must complete these tasks, but in an ever-increasing narcissistic culture, as many as twenty per week may evolve.

One solution is for the staff member to have a Web page outlining plans for the week. This solution provides an opportunity for the staff member to say, "I have all my plans on the Web, and here is the Web address. Feel free to check it at any time to get all the information you need." Again, this is an example of *professionally* sending some of the responsibility back to the parent, and this electronic syllabus is completed one time as op-posed to signing multiple agenda books or notes. Experience has shown that if even *one* note or signature is forgotten by a staff member, this in-cident becomes the issue brought to the table if the student continues to do poorly. Unfortunately—in line with the previously discussed "Clinton" justification—the student did not do the work, the parent did not hold the student accountable, but the educator forgot one slip, and this potentially is the item for debate.

Further, many schools now employ electronic grading systems to allow parents to check student progress at any time without badgering individual staff members. Staff members can embrace this type of system, as it again al-lows for a shift of responsibility *back* to the parent. If educators do not begin to shift tasks to the other participants in a child's education (parents and students), the list of teacher tasks continues to grow. Even though initial training and a learning curve for the staff exists, the new system ultimately simplifies some of their responsibilities.

5. When dealing with parents, educators must perpetually convey the message that all importance is placed on one issue—student learning. Situations that arise are not opportunities for finger pointing—it is *not* about parenting skills (or lack thereof). Even if the parent or home situation is partially responsible for shortcomings, the child is best helped by learning to adapt in spite of this condition. Therefore, school staff should focus on what the child can do for success and what changes in placement, attitude, or accommodations need to take place.

To further illustrate this point, consider the following example. If a student has been misbehaving in class, be mindful of the reasons often associated with the misbehavior—lack of parental support in the home, student merely trying to get attention, psychological condition (e.g., attention deficit hyperactivity disorder, bipolar disorder, etc.), or influence of peers. Any of these reasons are potential legitimate influences on behavior, but each is also an example of an issue that may affect a child indefinitely. Therefore, the focus of conversation should address how these items affect the child's *learning* and what coping skills the parent and child should practice in reference to his education. Further, school personnel should address how these issues may affect the learning of *other* students and inform the parents of the responsibility the school has in correcting the child's behaviors for the benefit of all learners, the teacher, and the child in question.

6. Especially in older students, educators must begin to stress and teach students the need for self-reliance. During the self-esteem movement, a perpetual "Are you happy?" approach was evident. Teachers were (and still are) criticized if school was "boring or hard." A systematic approach must allow students to realize that society does not revolve around their happiness or concerns, and students need to see the "larger picture." The approach should be tailored to the individual school building or district and include methods to educate the parents regarding proper school involvement, methods to prepare staff to converse with narcissistic individuals, and methods to encourage self-reliance on the part of the student-learner. Students can be empowered by realizing their successes and by discerning that satisfaction begins and ends ultimately with them.

This suggestion is *not* a justification for teachers to avoid differentiation of instruction, creative lesson plans, or active student engagement. If this assumption is made, it is erroneously made. However, students must realize no person (adult or child) ever truly learned anything without effort. In fact, it should be stated that the true measure of a person's education lies not in what they were taught, but rather in what they learned by their own accord. The classroom is an effective teaching arena to illustrate that the sum is more important than the parts, and students are individually part of the class just as citizens are part of society.

7. Community service projects are another excellent approach to teaching students the concept of assisting others and to realizing more important issues exist than simply their happiness. However, educators are encouraged to use caution. Simply mandating volunteerism as a graduation requirement or exploiting volunteerism to fulfill a personal agenda is hypocritical. In an era of public education bashing, schools have routinely used student service projects to take advantage of the public relations aspect of these endeavors. While this is understandable, if students are honored in the paper or on the evening news, or if they are encouraged to participate because these activities "look good on a resume for college or scholarships," all of the *real* education is lost.

One could take the position that in today's American society "activism is the new narcissism," and this can indeed be the case if students are simply volunteering to build resumes, garner media attention, or compete for awards. In a program where students can personally gain something concrete from helping others, narcissistic attitudes are being fostered. This "look at me" approach to philanthropy is self-absorbed, attention-seeking, and self-serving. People with these attitudes simply want the "press" for completing good deeds rather than attention for the cause they are "serving."

One suggestion for altering community service projects is to elaborate on student involvement and ownership in the project. For instance, rather than simply making a general requirement for the completion of community service, consider challenging students to research local families, organizations, or groups that need volunteers' support. After considering several options, students could select a premise for their project; their goal may be stamping out hunger, loneliness, homelessness, illiteracy, or any other valued cause.

After posing the premise, the students could then select the individuals or group they may help and take an active interest in meeting their proposed challenge. The students could also have the opportunity to select the manner in which they plan to assist the group. Throughout, students should be given time to reflect on their experiences and the degree to which their endeavors were successful. In addition to providing a record of participation for the staff member, a written reflection encourages students to evaluate their impact on others and their potential for further service opportunities. Their service should be seen as more meaningful than simply a graduation requirement to check off the list.

Lastly—and this may be debated on some levels—educators should avoid the urge to overly involve the media or press. Many educators follow the natural mindset to reward altruistic and acceptable behaviors with positive reinforcement. Our suggestion to avoid the press for community service projects is not meant to imply that positive reinforcement indicates poor practice or bad decision making (quite the contrary, we agree with positive reinforcement), but volunteerism is an arena that requires students do the right thing simply because it is the right thing to do. If students receive fame, glory, or accolades for helping others, the emphasis and distraction of the extrinsic motivators may lead to future actions that are less altruistic and more narcissistic in nature.

8. Because adults can similarly exhibit "service narcissism," school personnel should exercise caution when utilizing parents or community supporters. With certain people, this support may result in a larger debt at a later time. These individuals typically expect something in return for their actions and attempt to use the list of deeds completed for the school as "favor currency" when they have needs to be met.

The following brief list of considerations should be taken into account when utilizing parent or community volunteers:

- Limit the use of one particular parent or community member. Large accessibility in the building can lead to a greater sense of importance and entitlement.
- When volunteers enter the building, they should have concrete, clear, and precise instructions outlining their purpose for attending. If volunteers are free to roam about and interact as a staff member, they are more likely to engage in faculty discussions and leave with a greater sense of importance.
- Meet with volunteers and share any concerns or expectations *before* their tenure in the building. Taking the extra time to establish "ground rules" for behavior and roles pays dividends in the end.
- Avoid engaging the spouse, siblings, or close acquaintances of those in positions of importance in the district for volunteer duties. For example, the spouse of a board member could possibly already possess a sense of entitlement or feelings of over-importance; inviting him or her into the building as an extension of the school *could* potentially exacerbate the problem.

Ideally, volunteer duties should be done with a "no-strings-attached" mentality. Putting in extra time and consideration in filling volunteer positions may prevent awkward situations down the road.

9. Schools *must* cease the practice of providing signs, banners, or awards for every insignificant activity. Many of today's youth receive and expect

rewards for simply participating or "showing up," and narcissistic youths or parents protest vehemently if they or their children do not receive some recognition or extrinsic reward. Humility should be honored and encouraged.

A conscious effort must be put forth to return to truly honoring *exceptional* behavior, rather than what is expected for every other student. Awards designed to honor excellence and achievement are abundant and occur for a variety of reasons. As a result of the self-esteem movement, steps have been taken by many to ensure every participant in their particular groups receive *something*, serving as a tool for fostering positive self-esteem. Unfortunately, these students, potentially, come to expect this "something for participation" the rest of their lives, and many institutions are scrambling to address this mentality.

In fact, according to Fogarty (2008), children receive an average of 300 toys per year! Initially, most parents would likely deny that their child falls into that category, but when they consider each Happy Meal toy, birthday party goodie bag treat, holiday gifts, dentist rewards, and shopping splurges, the toys add up rather quickly (much to the pleasure of various toy companies). Granted, in some of the mentioned situations, the toys are not linked to the child being rewarded. Nevertheless, they do still feed the mentality of always receiving something. Eventually, when children are bombarded with "treats," they end up with so much *stuff* that most of it loses all value and importance to the owner. Children should feel just as much gratitude in receiving a sincere compliment as they should a ribbon or medal for a job well done.

10. Similarly, when a school district does design an awards program, it is crucial that the staff develop clear, specific criteria and maintain adherence to those criteria. Many schools now have numerous awards for students, and often, students who were "so close" to receiving awards are given leniency in the stated criteria. It is not an honor to qualify or receive an award if another person receives the same award for doing less.

Several examples of this exist, but perhaps the greatest is in the ever-popular, traditional "perfect attendance" award. Schools need to examine those students who actually receive this award. By definition, perfect attendance translates into *perfection*—no absences. How often does this really take place? For instance, many schools rule that students can receive the award if any absence was for death of a family member, college visitation, school-related absence, or medically-excused absence.

This is not a condemnation of those policies, but how much of an honor is a perfect attendance award if the person receiving the award missed 12 days in a 180-day school year? Obviously, one of the reasons schools allow all the exceptions is due to the challenges of the students and parents with narcissistic mindsets. They feel as though they are being punished if they don't receive the award. In other words, they feel entitled to have the recognition and indignant if it is not received. As the school personnel faces public scrutiny for not understanding poor Johnny's plight, they become leery of providing the award at all. Holding fast to criteria is the only proper manner to teach children they will not receive every award, incentive, or bonus, and that being happy for those who do receive the rewards is the best reaction to their disappointment.

11. In general, educators must reflect on their own actions taken and words used regarding student motivation and achievement. Often, a great deal of hypocrisy exists. Many educators have told students to "get your education so you can get a great job, make lots of money, and get lots of stuff!" Again, this logic feeds the narcissistic, consumer-driven culture. For years, stores have sold posters displaying mansions, fancy cars, and beautiful sunsets with the caption, "Justification for Higher Education." While this does indeed motivate many students, consider the shallow message being sent. Would a poster with Jonas Salk and the caption, "Study hard—cure a disease!" be less motivation? Presumably, yes—but it would be more beneficial to the educational cause and society at large.

12. Piggybacking on the previous suggestion, educators must resist the urge to add to the ever-growing grocery list of *extrinsic* motivation. Instead, they need to frequently reinforce the idea to students to do their best simply for the pride in knowing a job was done well with no tangible rewards provided. In actuality, this concept is quite rare in today's parenting formulas, and many schools have followed suit.

This type of motivation taking place in many school districts across the country ranges from simply providing candy for correct answers or completing homework to financially *paying* students for attendance. Perpetually feeding the narcissistic culture does not further the cause of education; rather, it hampers the personal teacher/student relationships that should form if student achievement is to take place. Students who inherently take pride in their work consistently perform better during school years and beyond. They also are more likely to persevere through long-term projects and goals without looking for immediate feedback or reward for every productive move. Such self-directed work habits are valuable in any work environment. Frankly, programming students to work only for reward is cruel, as most students never encounter a similar working environment beyond their school days.

13. Regardless of the need for operating revenues, educators should remove commercial advertising from the school setting, as it so often encour-

ages the narcissistic lifestyle. Students are inundated with, "You need this to be beautiful," or "This makes you the person you deserve to be." Schools should provide a break from this commercialism.

Children face countless celebrity images, and numerous companies market and attempt to capitalize on this type of promotion. From "Got Milk?" celebrity ads to numerous localized photography studios reinforcing the need for the best senior pictures, students are continually told they deserve only the best in life. These messages reinforce the idea that individual students are the center of the universe, and "life is good when they receive their just deserts."

14. Educators should consider developing curriculum, assessment, and coursework that foster student reflection on the connection between their work ethic and their efforts in relation to their successes. An example of assessment is a music instructor requiring a "practice log" for tracking student growth in the instrumental music setting.

As stated previously, lying and embellishment are traditional characteristics of self-absorbed behavior; obviously, these behaviors may be tried by some. However, it becomes difficult to hide behind falsely reported hours spent practicing a skill if little success is exhibited when asked to perform that skill. Granted, educators must recognize individual learning differences in determining expected levels of success. However, if adequate time on studying, practicing, or preparing is being reported and a student is still failing, most likely the student is lying, or this discrepancy may be an indication of a learning disability. In these cases, follow-up by the staff should be done.

Students need opportunities to make the connection between their effort and successes (or lack thereof). In most cases, teachers can reasonably project the performance expected from a specific degree of effort, and these factors can effectively be connected in students' grades.

15. In a similar manner as described previously, educators can teach students the concepts of narcissism, as well as humility, philanthropy, and teamwork. These concepts should be directly addressed, and students should understand how these ideas are applicable to their development as citizens and growth as healthy, well-adjusted adults. It is important for students to understand the positive aspects of good self-esteem, but they also need to understand what implications exist if they are developing in a narcissistic, overindulged household. Students should understand we all have varying degrees of narcissism, but they should be able to distinguish between a healthy, confident individual versus the unhealthy narcissist incapable of having sustainable personal relationships.

Many of these lessons come with choosing curriculum wisely. All language arts courses at every level require some form of reading and study of the written word. Careful selection of literature can provide prime opportunities for discussions of character. For example, choosing titles such as *A Christmas Carol*, which highlights the consequences of narcissistic behavior, assists in this goal. For older students, *The Great Gatsby* chronicles the dark side of the American Dream and the shallow personality that accompanies such a selfish, overindulgent lifestyle. In all grade levels, literature portraying the plight of the narcissistic individual can be used. Any story that requires self-reflection and depicts the negative consequences of the narcissistic way of life sends a positive message to students.

In addition to the study of literature that examines these characteristics, students should be encouraged to study individuals who have devoted themselves to others freely without the intent of becoming famous. Individuals such as Gandhi and Mother Teresa epitomize working for those less fortunate and devoting their lives to altruistic endeavors. In completing projects on biographies and autobiographies, students could be required to read about an individual based on that premise.

Further, students could examine and research people in their own neighborhoods, searching for those individuals "close to home" who have exhibited selflessness as well. Often these individuals carry respect from the citizens in the area. Realizing the respect given to these individuals should further reinforce the message of the benefits of selfless behavior.

16. Educators could create learning situations where students must "stand on their own two feet" and handle conflict independently. Of course, this is not to undermine a child's safety. However, students should be allowed to apply and develop strategies to successfully resolve issues that arise, addressing the following questions: What approaches should I take? How do I speak to authority figures? What social skills am I lacking that lead to my involvement in these conflicts? Whom should I contact should I need assistance? These are issues and concepts that could develop naturally for all children, given enough freedom and autonomy to discover them on their own time through their own merits.

Parents and school officials alike must be prepared to address the lack of emotional growth, which undoubtedly occurs should students have controlling adults providing direction for every situation that occurs on a daily basis. It is impossible to tell parents to "stop battling for their child" without alienating the parent. However, an acceptable approach would be to state to a parent, "Let's show Johnny what it feels like to handle a situation on his own and gain a sense of empowerment. He feels better about himself when he realizes that he can come to the office on his own, as he recognizes he took steps to solve the problem."

As with many other topics in education, the delivery is the key. Telling parents to stay away creates adversarial relationships; asking for their assistance in empowering their child and teaching independence is met with much greater support. Choosing the right words is paramount in dealing with this issue in the school setting.

17. To truly make long-lasting impacts, school personnel could strive to educate the families in their district. Educators could create an opportunity to begin dialogue with the parents regarding their *proper* role in the educational setting. Ideally, these types of initiatives may be best suited at the elementary level, as this tends to be the time when parents are the most receptive to parenting and teaching techniques.

Nevertheless, the attempts could be made with parents at all levels when students first enter various buildings in the educational process. For example, orientation programs typically take place when students enter the elementary, middle, and high school levels. These are prime moments to perpetually send the message of how successful parents can mentor their children and modify the parents' level of involvement according to the development and maturation of the child. The message that needs to be reinforced to parents is that it is acceptable to allow students to develop relationships with school personnel and even respectfully discuss their concerns with those individuals when appropriate.

Further, parents need to realize that sometimes their primary role for their disgruntled child is to simply listen. Amazingly, people often feel less upset or even alter their perception after simply "venting" about a situation. Too often, the parent uses the "rush to action" approach discussed previously and attempts to fix the problem for the student. If the child's safety is not at risk, listening to a child and providing suggestions and guidance are often the best approach. As children mature, these are valuable tools, which add to the development of the student learner.

Some educators may scoff at the idea of having a "new program" or initiative to institute. This resistance is understandable and, in many cases, justified. However, this step should actually be used to decrease the workload of many educators. Parents who begin to "pull back" in their overindulgence are more likely to have a healthy relationship with the district, and their child may actually achieve more in the classroom. It is a simple premise: do a little work "up front" and notice the benefits, or sit back and watch the population of narcissistic, overindulged children grow and demand more work later. The "servant" attitude of the narcissistic parent is exhausting; eliminating this perception is necessary for all stakeholders in the learning continuum.

18. Educators should frequently provide "real-world" facts as students explore future plans and careers. Allowing children to "dream" is important, but if their dreams are unrealistic, failure is inevitable. A more responsible approach to helping children plan their futures is to combine dreams with reality.

At all grade levels, as students share ideas about college and career choices, educators can provide data to give students a realistic picture of what it takes to reach their goals. The amount and types of data should be varied by the age of the students. For example, an elementary student may share that he wants to be a veterinarian because he loves animals. An activity or discussion should then take place, sharing how many years of schooling are required to be a veterinarian and what academic subject areas are stressed in that particular career.

In providing this data, the idea is for the educator to have the students reflect on simple connections between themselves and their desired career. Therefore, the next step should be to have students reflect on their current behaviors related to the shared data: How well do they like school? Do they have good attendance? What grades do they have in the courses related to their chosen career? What can they do to help make their dreams realistic? All of this data is fairly simple, yet it provides important information to reinforce that effort, accomplishments, and learned work habits (even at a young age) are directly connected to future achievement.

With older students, more specific data should be evaluated. For instance, after the first grade point averages are established for high school students, school personnel could share an overview of admission requirements for various colleges, focusing primarily on local colleges and ones commonly attended by students in that district. The data could include ACT and SAT scores, grade point averages, course requirements, and other factors that determine admission acceptance. Again, the educator should encourage the students to make meaningful connections between their academic performances to that point of their career and requirements for potential goals.

Without these opportunities to enlighten students, those with narcissistic tendencies often believe they are able to succeed in any career simply because they *want* that. They fail to see that desire must manifest itself as hard work, tenacity, and achievement. Ultimately, these students face a higher failure rate because they have not learned what it takes to work toward goals successfully.

19. Speak frankly when addressing narcissistic parents and students. This suggestion requires caution and tact. In fact, if school personnel are not

capable of exhibiting these traits in the face of conflict, this strategy is best not used—as using this strategy ineffectively causes more stress and harm than good. However, many (not all) parents listen and take heart when information regarding their child or their behavior is received from a *trusted* individual. It is with this motive that school personnel are advised to pull the parent aside and state, "(parent's name) I have tried to help you on this occasion (and list all the moments), and I have tried this strategy (list all strategies), and I simply cannot afford to spend every waking moment addressing so many issues—you must begin to assist us in the process of educating your child."

A simple example of dealing with the narcissistic parent is similar to a rule for dealing with stray cats and dogs that may appear in your neighborhood: "If you feed it, it is yours." Many educators have succumbed to addressing the needs of the narcissistic parent only to discover that those needs are never fully met. These parents have perpetual "issues" that need attention, and this parent may make statements such as, "No one seems to care or want to help me with my child" when in reality, more attention has been given to this child than many students in the class or the school. Encouraging their requests is problematic as it reinforces the message to continually bring personal problems into the school environment.

These conversations can only take place after the teacher, counselor, or administrator has worked with the family for a length of time. Attempting to have this conversation prior to offering the first avenue of assistance would not be prudent and, in fact, may be negligent; not every parent with an "issue" is exhibiting narcissistic characteristics. However, after the staff member has devoted considerable time laying the foundation of trust, the conversations become easier, and under the premise of empowerment for the child, progress can be made.

20. The last suggestion to combat this issue in the school setting falls on school personnel. Educators would benefit by reflecting on the initial nineteen suggestions provided, initiating any and all that fit the individual circumstances relevant to their positions and continue to dialogue, converse, and brainstorm other methods to address these concerns. As this topic is discussed with other members of the profession, most educators find that others feel the same. Healthy (non-complaining) conversation and dialogue can serve two purposes. First, it is therapeutic for educators to know that others feel the way they do and they are not alone. Secondly, ideas arrive from these discussions and creative ideas are powerful measures to address any problem facing public education today.

As great solutions often remain to be discovered, this chapter is not meant to imply that the preceding list is the guaranteed "cure all" for many of the narcissistic effects plaguing America's educational system today. However, this chapter does stand out to us as quite possibly the most important chapter in the publication, as simply identifying a problem doesn't provide significant value to improving conditions. Extensive and frequent effort must be shown among educators if the proverbial pendulum is to swing toward an educational system that requires greater independence on the part of the learner and places more emphasis on the idea of living, learning, and working for the "greater good."

CHAPTER NINE

∽

Understanding and Addressing the Narcissistic Point of View

From time to time, meetings with angry parents, unsupportive administration, and misinformed policy makers occur that require the articulation necessary to address how significant and widespread narcissistic ways of thinking have become. It is in this vein that this chapter's thoughts are provided to support the proper position regarding parenting, education, and mentoring children to become healthy adults capable of sustaining successful relationships.

Remember, individuals with narcissistic tendencies often resist any logic that is contrary to their opinion or position on an issue. A key to effective communication between people at odds is to bridge the gap separating the viewpoints. Taking time to understand how a narcissistic individual's realities are created and reinforced provides insight that may prove strategic and beneficial in building this bridge.

As explained in the discussion of acquired situational narcissism in an earlier chapter, conditions in our daily lives can potentially exacerbate narcissistic tendencies. For example, excessive opportunities for attention or the fear of losing someone or something important may ignite behaviors symptomatic of narcissism. Many other situations that lead to an increase in a narcissistic, self-absorbed mindset have been discussed throughout this text. In our current culture, these situations are prominent—even inescapable. Thus, as educators prepare to effectively communicate with parents, students, and colleagues with narcissistic tendencies, it is important to review the issues that amplify narcissistic behaviors or attitudes. Through an increased understanding of what provokes narcissistic individuals' thoughts or behaviors, a productive approach to confront these individuals can be learned.

Factors Facilitating the Narcissistic Mindset

1. News-Based Media
Potentially Narcissistic-Provoking Messages:

- "Every parent's nightmare" occurs at least once a day around the world.
- Parents must protect their children from endless threats: predators, poisonous toys from foreign countries, perverted teachers and clergy, tainted food, bullying and harassment from peers, killer bees, pandemic viruses, and so on.
- In order to be protected in our world, trust few and fear many.

Possible Narcissistic Manifestation:

Parents in the United States face frequent news stories where fear or anxiety is the consequence of the update. While a culture of fear may not be a direct link or correlation to narcissistic thinking, it can very well lend itself to overprotective parenting styles that focus all attention to the mere preservation of the child. This "protectionist" approach provides for a greater emphasis on the child as the center of the family. When parents believe their child is the center of their life and they must protect their child from nearly all others, they think and act with a narrow focus.

As discussed in a previous chapter, the focus of any family unit should be on the relationships among its members. When the focus intensifies and shifts to the individual child's constant needs, overindulgence often follows. An important distinction should be made between the preservation of family versus the preservation of individual family members when developing family values. Narcissistic individuals often do not make that distinction.

This point is not meant to imply that safety and well-being are not important factors in the growth and development of a child. In fact, one could easily argue health and safety are the primary responsibilities of the parents in any setting. While this fact is undeniably true, any form of protection can be taken to extreme levels, and extreme levels of anything can lead to negative consequences. A protect-at-all-cost mentality can lead to a retardation of child development. This retardation is exacerbated when the school is the focus of the protectionist mindset, and as many educators are aware, this way of thinking is an increasing trend.

2. Internet Usage
Potentially Narcissistic-Provoking Messages:

- Anyone can achieve fame—I should too.
- Those individuals who are the most outrageous and daring are the most admired.
- The more exposure or "hits" I have online, the more worthy I am.
- The desire for personal privacy is an old-fashioned concept.

Possible Narcissistic Manifestation:

Social Websites can have a useful place in our society, serving as a method to stay in contact with friends, professional acquaintances, or even former students, but the potential for profound negative consequences to the larger group also exists. When children or adults can instantly have thousands of perceived "fans" and achieve the fame sought by so many in the American culture, the negative aspects of the narcissistic mindset often emerge. These individuals may not understand why behaviors so admired and coveted on the Internet are not admired (or even approved of) in every setting.

Further, when people engage in activities they believe will lead to fame or notoriety, they should question, "For what am I going to be noticed, celebrated, or remembered?" Often individuals have not thought through the permanence of their exploits and may not realize that their postings could affect important aspects of their lives such as their college acceptance, future or current careers, or even their legal records.

When fame is sought for the sake of fame itself, an erosion of character takes place. People who place great emphasis on approval from others get trapped in a cycle of trying to attain that approval constantly for self-worth. To them, it is more important to be known and respected by others than to have a sincere self-respect. They may be more likely to compromise their values and morals, as long as it means impressing someone else. Self-affirmation is equated with approval and recognition from others in this attention-seeking mindset.

3. Self-Esteem Education Movement
Potentially Narcissistic-Provoking Messages:

- Self-esteem develops in isolation; simply telling someone he or she is special will build a healthy self-esteem.
- Children should *always* feel good about themselves, no matter what.
- Good parents protect their children from feeling negative emotions.

Possible Narcissistic Manifestation:

Education must take some responsibility for the increase in narcissistic tendencies. While the self-esteem movement is grounded in good intentions, the consequences of promoting self-esteem before accomplishment are shortsighted and counterproductive. As a result, a parenting and educational undertow has espoused that if children are made to feel special, they will ultimately be more special.

Of course, parents want their children to be confident and happy. However, while the goal of a healthy, self-actualized individual is important in educating a child, false self-esteem can potentially have a more detrimental effect than no self-esteem. An undergrounded sense of self will often lead to an inflated ego—one of the hallmarks of the narcissistic personality.

For years, many adults have been fed half-truths and misconceptions about how to help their children develop a healthy self-esteem. Educators and parents alike must perpetually be cognizant of how building children up to motivate them to perform can affect their future growth. Often this excessive encouragement translates into an individual who expects to be "built up" again so they will achieve again. Many adults have not considered how children will react when no one is there to do that building up as a precursor for action.

4. Focus on Aesthetics and Beauty
Potentially Narcissistic-Provoking Messages:

- Physical perfection is attainable.
- Physical beauty equates with success, wealth, happiness, and so on.
- As long as I'm beautiful, people will listen to me and respond to my needs.
- When I don't get what I want from others, their failure to cooperate is due to jealousy.

Possible Narcissistic Manifestation:

As discussed previously, American culture is showered with advertising addressing the inherent benefits of looking better or being perceived as attractive. The average person finds it impossible to become totally immune to the explicit messages supporting these claims.

While a message of exercise, eating right, or taking steps to remain healthy are reasonable suggestions for anyone, constant images of beauty and focus on one's physical appearance can be counterproductive to a healthy personality, self-concept, and relationships. Following the common adage that "beauty is only skin deep," a person's ability to contribute to society should be determined by so much more than his or her body size or facial features. Individuals who become preoccupied with their appearance versus their capabilities are selling themselves short. They may not see the value in developing their talents and abilities when they've come to believe success should come with beauty.

Further, people who view themselves as attractive may expect preferential treatment from others based on that perception alone. After all, they have been promised as much time and time again through advertising: beauty means power and influence. As discussed previously, successful advertising campaigns are designed to be individualized to each of us. A constant barrage of media directed to feed the need of the individual consumer is bound to increase a sense of self-perception and influence his or her expectation of others' responses.

5. Current Parenting Perceptions
Potentially Narcissistic-Provoking Messages:

- The ideal childhood is free of harm, criticism, and hardship.
- Today's parents must raise their children differently than they themselves were raised.
- Parents' primary responsibility is to ensure their child's happiness.

Possible Narcissistic Manifestation:

Understandably, parents want more for their children than they had. Often, their reactions to situations are motivated by those intentions. Previously, research was cited that identified a parent's primary determinant of a quality teacher to be their child's happiness in class. While happiness is an emotion for which we all strive, one should not lose sight of the negative consequences of individuals making the majority of their decisions based on the search for perpetual happiness. Again, an excessive focus on the individual's needs is at the core of the narcissistic mindset.

Further, as the American family lifestyle is often hectic and fast-paced, the last thing many parents want to face in their limited bonding time is an unhappy child. Thus, many parents, out of guilt or obligation, feel the need to take any steps necessary to add to their child's happiness. Again, their child receives the indirect message that his happiness is paramount in the mission of his parents and may even come to *expect* undivided devotion and attention to his needs.

Parents that feel obligated to keep their children happy at all costs commonly protect them from humbling experiences or avenues of failure, as they fear potential damages to a healthy psyche. One must not forget the valuable lessons potentially learned from failure. When a child escapes experiences of failure during early maturation, he loses the opportunity to develop coping skills for working through those experiences, which become inevitable as life proceeds. Further, individuals protected from failure potentially develop an inflated sense of self if they have only experienced success over an extended period of life. Overall, perpetually steering children away from humbling experiences not only prevents growth but may lead to self-absorbed, inflated egos.

6. Decline in Traditional Family Norms and Values
Potentially Narcissistic-Provoking Messages:

- Personal enjoyment, pleasure, and satisfaction are the keys to a good life.
- In previous generations, many people's lives had very little true meaning.
- Personal beliefs supersede beliefs associated with organizations, religions, government agencies, and so on.

Possible Narcissistic Manifestation:

The focus on this factor is not meant as a call for a return to the past ways of life. Those calls are nearly impossible to meet, and truly, the perceptions of a past era are sometimes more positive than the reality. However, one characteristic of many people (adults and students) of contemporary America is a lack of loyalty to ideas or groups larger than ourselves. For example, some millennials (those people born between the years 1980–1995) strive to live differently than their parents. After watching their parents toil and struggle, these individuals have committed to adopting a different lifestyle.

While wanting better than our parents is a staple of American society, the justifications for wanting more have changed. The notion that previous generations successfully completed lifelong careers solely out of obligation to the workplace is just part of the story. Much of the obligation to endure was for family survival. For that generation, an ideal existed above self-happiness that drove their actions. Participation in organized religion, community service groups, and planned family gatherings was also more common and perceived as valuable time spent.

In modern society, individuals are encouraged to "look out for number one" and to customize their lives for personal satisfaction. One of the characteristics of narcissism is the expectation of special treatment and seeing oneself as better than others. Individuals with these tendencies will expect institutions, such as school systems, to customize operations to suit their needs. Often, these individuals believe they or their children should be considered exceptions to the rules and, consequently, should be treated preferentially.

While the preceding list is not meant to be all-inclusive, it does serve as a reference for the growth of the narcissistic culture in the United States. In considering the power these factors have on shaping the views of people, educators may begin to better understand the tainted logic and misconceptions of narcissistic individuals. The ability to empathize with their need to preserve themselves or their loved ones creates trust and a common ground. Once the trust is established, educators have a greater chance of influencing the mindset of the narcissistic thinker. Throughout the discussion, educators should stress the mutual concern of serving the student's best educational interests repeatedly and directly explain how the educators' opinions and actions serve this purpose.

As a starting point, the following statements can be used when attempting to successfully enforce policy and guidelines of the classroom, building, or district. As exhausting as this task may be, combating the sense of entitlement of the self-absorbed is necessary and productive in the long-term operations of the school system. You are encouraged to use your own arguments, but the following conversation points may provide some necessary direction in addressing these individuals and their concerns.

1. No child, especially a teenager, should be given anything if the child is expected to appreciate and value what he or she has been afforded.
This has been proven time and again. A teenager is given a car and drives like a maniac; a teenager is given half the money for a car and earns the rest and drives with care, as he takes greater pride in the effort put forth to acquire the vehicle. The same can be said in the classroom. The student who is given something initially in hopes of motivating the student has little incentive for achievement; the student who is rewarded for success takes great pride in the accomplishment. Schools should work with students, finding the correct "buttons" to push for incentives to be successful, and when at all possible, choosing the incentives that reward work for the greater good rather than individual good.

2. For any organization to be successful, at some point, those individuals who believe they are the exception must conform to the policies rather than the policies addressing all the exceptions.
This applies to every rule in every handbook across the country. For every district or building policy in place, individuals who believe they are entitled

to an exception can be named. This "free pass" way of thinking is destroying the fabric of our organizations and creating an over-reliance on institutions. In fact, in many districts, it is more common to be an exception rather than part of the general population. This has created a tremendous burden on the school and the taxpayer as this has increased the amount of personnel needed to address all the possible student scenarios entering the building on a daily basis.

Districts should hold fast and ensure *all* students have equal access, equal opportunity, and equal accountability. It is important to note that for every exception, a loss of accountability occurs. Knowing and understanding how to be accountable is a vital piece for student success after formal schooling has ended.

3. "The worst thing you can do for those you love is the things they could do and should do for themselves." (John Wooden [1997, p. 199], former UCLA Hall of Fame basketball coach, quoting Abraham Lincoln)

This concept is directly related to the topic of putting students in situations where they can and should learn the coping skills necessary for success. If every parent rushed to the school demanding an apology for every challenging comment made to their child, the halls would be full of parents, and the meetings would effectively end all instruction. The adults who work with children (parents and school personnel alike) are best involved when they provide a sounding board, an opportunity for students to discuss the day's events, and guiding advice. Mentoring parents understand this. Mentoring parents *suggest* rather than handle, they *encourage* rather than take over, and they often *listen* rather than voice concerns.

4. An education without effort is insufficient at best.

Too often, students attend school with the attitude that the teacher is there to "learn me." The term "learn me" was carefully chosen, as a grave difference is implied between "me learning" and someone "learning me." Students are sent to school to learn; teachers are to facilitate and instruct. While this may seem elementary in thinking, apparently some fundamental facets of this concept have been lost along the way.

Teaching is more than deliverance of curriculum—it always has been. It is inspiration, coercion, prodding, pleading, and instructing. But the child *must* be an *active* participant. Countless meetings have been had with students who did not study, prepare, attend tutoring sessions, complete assignments, or raise questions in class when they were confused, but then complained that the staff member "taught me nothing." At least the phrase, "I *learned* nothing in that class" ensures that the child acknowledges at least fifty percent of the responsibility for the "I did not learn anything" cry.

As adults, we know that countless professional development time and money is wasted if the employee (regardless of the profession) refuses to participate in the learning process. Too often, we allow children to escape the accountability expected of adults even though we know that the accountability piece is present as a child matures. This is truly a mistake and ultimately unfair to a child's development.

5. You cannot be self-absorbed with narcissistic tendencies and ever have lasting happiness!

Hopefully, at this point in the text, the message is clear that many of the individuals who possess these tendencies are never truly happy and never experience lasting pleasure with their lives. These individuals are often cynical of others and never truly feel as though they have fully gotten their just rewards.

Knowing this and not addressing the students who exhibit these characteristics as they mature is wrong and presents an almost certain recipe for an unfulfilling adult life. As difficult as these individuals may be, the failure to address their behaviors is not conducive to their learning or the success of the building. Narcissism is a battle that must be addressed.

6. "Ask not what your country can do for you; ask what you can do for your country." (John F. Kennedy, former president of the United States)

This statement is one of the most popular and recognized speech excerpts among Americans. But how often is it truly acted upon? Unlike years gone by, the majority of Americans' daily lives can be rather comfortable with little effort. Daily survival, food, and shelter typically are not questioned, and our comfort often turns into complacency.

Obviously, such luxurious living does not exist for all Americans or in all countries. Students need to realize that safe, comfortable living is not a given, and that each member of any community is vital to its continuing existence. From a very young age, students should be encouraged to recognize their value in their community and learn to contribute their worth.

As these six guiding statements are analyzed, it is important to stress that they are provided not simply to serve as comebacks to "win" an argument with a narcissistic individual. Ultimately, each of the ideas stems from true concern for fostering healthy development in our school-aged citizens. This underlying motive must be stressed so parents and students understand educators' reason to redirect students. In any successful program of change, in addition to identifying the undesirable, it is as important (and likely more important) to identify the desired outcome.

When attempting to squelch narcissistic tendencies, educators are ultimately striving to teach and encourage basic principles and values that help students become well-adjusted, happy, productive adults. The resistance to "give in" to immediate demands may create opportunities to teach valuable lessons. For example, the six ideas listed here encourage the following characteristics, respectively: appreciation, adaptability and conformity, self-reliance, industriousness, contentedness, and civic responsibility.

Not so coincidentally, these values resemble some of the most basic principles on which our country and our earliest school systems were founded. Although the world has changed in countless ways since the early years of our nation's existence, these qualities have proven to be timeless. Regardless of changes in technology and communication, the national economy, foreign relations, or conveniences and challenges in life, fostering qualities in students to help them reach their full potential for themselves and those around them is a constant for success.

CHAPTER TEN

~

An Examination of Case Studies

After reviewing each of the chapters regarding narcissism and analyzing its impact on the daily operations of the educational setting, it is important that you, the reader, reflect on your position and how this text can assist your interactions with the constituents you serve. Following the most basic of educational principles, the next challenge is to successfully implement the new strategies in your day-to-day positions. The following scenarios have been presented for further reflection and practice as you attempt to address the behaviors and characteristics that affect the personnel in your individual buildings.

As time permits, role-play the scenarios with another staff member. One individual should take the role of the narcissistic, self-absorbed parent, student, or staff member who refuses to "take no" for an answer. The other staff member should take on the role of the school personnel charged with meeting with this narcissistic individual. As this is a role-play situation, the stress associated with meeting is decreased, and an opportunity for growth is provided.

Further, this type of development allows both individuals to gain experience in understanding the verbal arguments these individuals use to make their points. In addition, both staff members begin to appreciate the stamina it takes to conduct such a meeting.

Scenario 1

Alex is a third-grade elementary student. His parents believe he is a highly talented vocalist and have even sent CDs to *American Idol* in hope of garnering some national attention. He has performed for the class at various times, and he is actually very average in his abilities. However, he has succumbed to his parents' barrage of accolades and believes he is destined for stardom.

The elementary talent show is quickly approaching, and Alex (and his parents) did not remember to sign the audition sheet for the show. Numerous reminders were announced and several flyers were sent home with students outlining the rules for auditioning. A small article appeared in the school newsletter as well. The deadline for sign-ups has come and gone, and several other parents have asked for exceptions to sign up late for a variety of reasons. All have been told "no" as it seemed unfair to choose which students had the right to garner such an exception.

Alex's parents request a meeting to discuss the matter as "the school would be better represented and the show would be better" if their son were allowed to showcase his talents.

Points to Ponder

As you role-play with your colleague, consider the arguments the parents use to justify their desire for an exception and answer the following questions.

- What parental justification should the teacher anticipate?
- Who will the parents believe is ultimately responsible for the failure to sign the audition sheet?
- What items should the school personnel provide during the course of the meeting?
- How will the parents react if they are told the deadline has passed and nothing can be done?

Scenario 2

Alyssa is a high school senior with two weeks left in her senior year. She is currently taking a required senior English course and has struggled to complete assignments or study for tests during the year. She passed the first semester with a D-, failed the third quarter, and now needs a passing grade in the last quarter to receive credit for the course. She has not done well in the fourth quarter either, missing several days of school, failing to turn in several assignments, and failing most of the assessments given by the instructor.

Her parents have been notified by phone of her poor progress on four occasions during the quarter, as well as by two letters sent home by mail. The teacher has offered to stay after school all year for struggling students, and Alyssa failed to attend any of these extra sessions. Lastly, Alyssa was given the opportunity to turn in late assignments for partial credit and failed to meet any of the secondary deadlines as well.

A meeting was scheduled after the instructor told Alyssa that she could not mathematically pass for the year and would need to take summer school courses. This failure also prohibits her from participating in the graduation ceremony. She and her parents are visibly upset as "they have family coming in from all over to celebrate the first child to graduate high school in their family."

Points to Ponder

- What requests should the educators in the meeting expect during the course of the conversation?
- What arguments should be anticipated in demanding these requests?
- What items (if any) should the school personnel provide during the meeting?
- Who is responsible for Alyssa and her situation? Why?
- Is it possible to prevent a situation like this from happening in the future?
- What stance should the school take in this situation?
- Does Alyssa's age and grade level change the situation for school personnel?

Scenario 3

John is a very good student and has never received any discipline referrals in all the years of his schooling. During class one day, his cell phone rang and interrupted the class discussion. The teacher confiscated the phone and reported John to the office (per building policy) for a two-hour Saturday School. Later, it was discovered that John's mother had called attempting to leave a voice mail about an after-school activity.

John was later called to the office and received his discipline referral. Just before the assistant principal was to leave for the day, the phone rang. It was John's mother, and she was upset. She was requesting a "few minutes of his time" to speak before he left for the evening.

Points to Ponder

- Why do you think his mother is upset with the school?
- What arguments do you think she will use to justify her position?

- Do you believe John deserves an exception to the cell phone rule? Why?
- How might this conversation affect the assistant principal's mood and evening?

Scenario 4

Emily is a junior high student and is often criticizing others and making them feel inferior. One particular student, Jackie, is perpetually the target of her verbal thrashings. After enduring this for several weeks, Jackie becomes frustrated and punches Emily in the mouth. Several staff and students make certain to provide insight to the principal in regard to Emily's demeanor and behavior in the school setting.

Per policy, Jackie is suspended for several days for a physical altercation, but the administration feels as though Emily's past behavior has led to this situation and decides to punish her as well. Emily's parents are infuriated that she received a punishment after being "assaulted" and demand a meeting, even threatening legal action.

Points to Ponder

- What is the position of the parents in this situation?
- What do you think Emily has told her parents of the situation prior to this event?
- What materials (if any) should the educators have in place when preparing for this meeting?
- How should the school administration handle this situation? Should both girls be punished?
- What will the position of Jackie's parents be in this situation?
- How should the administration handle the situation if both sets of parents are narcissistic and overindulgent?

Scenario 5

Alan is in high school and has filled out the application for acceptance into his school's chapter of the National Honor Society (NHS). He has been involved in numerous activities and has managed to perform at an above-average level in his academic coursework. He is considered a "nice guy" by his peers and the staff in the building, but is not viewed as "exceptional" by his teachers. His parents believe he is destined for an outstanding career and acceptance into the most prestigious college.

After careful consideration by the committee, he is not granted acceptance, and he is devastated by the news. His parents have demanded a meeting with the NHS advisor to discuss why he was not accepted into this prestigious academic group. They are frustrated that he is now going to be "shut out" of the best schools and no longer be eligible for scholarships. Further, they have incriminating "information" regarding many of the students who were chosen by the committee.

Points to Ponder

- What arguments will his parents provide for justification for their displeasure?
- How should the advisor handle the "attacks" on the other nominated members of the group?
- What do you think the parents hope to gain by such a meeting?
- How is this situation exacerbated if the parents hold positions of prestige in the community or in the school setting? What if one or both parents are on the teaching staff?
- Does the socioeconomic status of the family affect their arguments or the manner in which they behave during the meeting? If so, how?

Scenario 6

Bob is a faculty member of your school. He readily volunteers for professional committees, teaches quality lessons, and is a favorite among the student population and community members. However, he is frequently late to school or assigned duties, he often fails to meet administrative deadlines in academic reporting, and he is brazen in his criticism of those staff members who "do not pull their own weight."

Tense moments have surfaced in the past when administration or staff attempt to address Bob's shortcomings. Any effort to converse with him in this regard culminates in his anger at not acknowledging his contributions to the school and students. As a result, the staff avoids engaging in collegial discussions with him, and Bob views their avoidance as jealousy regarding his accomplishments and stature among the students and community.

Points to Ponder

- If you were Bob's administrator, would you address his behavior, attitude, and perceptions? If so, how? If not, why?

- If you were a colleague of Bob's, would you attempt to engage in a conversation with him regarding his beliefs or perceptions of his abilities and role in the building? If yes, how? If not, why?
- If the administration or a colleague were to address this issue with Bob, do you believe the discussion will have a lasting effect on his mindset? His behaviors?
- Would it be more beneficial if Bob were addressed (a) by the administration or (b) by a fellow staff member? Justify your selection.

The purpose of the scenarios is two-fold. First, they illustrate just how frustrating and exasperating it can be to anticipate and then endure some of the meetings with narcissistic parents whose sense of entitlement overshadows the need for school policy. Unfortunately, parental support is not the only support lacking in some cases. As some of these meetings can end in legal proceedings, the courts have at times also chosen to examine the wording of the rule as opposed to the need for maintaining order and discipline in the school setting.

Second, the scenarios illustrate the logical distortions that take place when the narcissistic student, parent, or school employee faces consequences for violation of any school rule. Most of these individuals, especially adults, understand the need for policies and rules, but they fail to understand that for any policy to be effective, it should be applied uniformly. Again, everyone wants rules, but most do not seem to want rules for themselves or their children.

Spending time understanding the mindset of narcissistic individuals certainly is advantageous for educators. Each experience (whether hypothetical or real) will prepare teachers and administrators to better handle the next situation. Because narcissistic individuals can be very demanding and narrow-minded, some educators may find it difficult to avoid reacting with obvious frustration. Preparation and practice prior to these encounters allow for a better chance of a professional reaction and a productive outcome for the meeting.

Conclusion and Recommended Readings

Throughout this publication, numerous illustrations regarding the effects, appearances, and characteristics of the self-absorbed, narcissistic learner are presented. Several possible variables are investigated and proposed as potential "causes" for the ever-increasing trend in these behavioral traits.

All in all, an apparent "perfect storm" of sophisticated advertising aimed at our self-interests, an increase in nouveau self-esteem-building parenting techniques that place the child at the center of the family and on equal footing with the adults, and technology that provides an inflated perception of "popularity" on the mental psyche of maturing adolescents has been brewing. As a result, the American student has changed in many ways regarding learning and achievement.

No doubt at this time it is possible to feel exhausted at the mere thought of dealing with narcissistic students, parents, staff, or administrators. Unfortunately, these individuals can be just that—draining and frustrating. However, understanding how these people think, reason, manipulate, and coerce is vital to surviving and functioning in this work environment.

This publication shall end where it began—with 15,000 publications regarding the importance of self-esteem. If one individual can begin such a movement, surely the hard work and dedication of a few can be the impetus for the steps necessary to begin changing this portion of educational history—indeed, changes that have become necessary for our students, our profession, and our society at large.

Recommended Readings

If the topic of narcissism is one of interest and something that inspires further study, we recommend the following titles as a good starting point:

Why Is It Always About You? The Seven Deadly Sins of Narcissism, Sandy Hotchkiss. An excellent source for examining the development of narcissism in people and for suggesting strategies on how to deal with narcissistic, self-indulged people in everyday life.

Generation Me: Why Today's Young Americans Are More Confident, Assertive, Entitled—and More Miserable Than Ever Before, Professor Jean Twenge, Ph.D. This publication closely examines the newest generation of Americans entering the workforce and adult life through all aspects of society. This is a lighthearted read about some serious issues and ramifications that are just beginning to become evident in American culture.

The Culture of Narcissism: American Life in an Age of Diminishing Expectations, Christopher Lasch. While written in 1971, this publication examines the societal ills and negative implications of widespread narcissism in a consumer-driven culture. Deeply thought-provoking and at times frightening, Lasch's work eloquently predicts much of America's present social crises and the role self-absorption plays in exacerbating each dilemma.

Children of the Self-Absorbed: A Grown-Up's Guide to Getting Over Narcissistic Parents, Nina Brown. Designed for assistance in dealing with the control narcissistic parents so deeply desire and attempt to exert on their children, this publication attempts to point out the steps people can take to free themselves of this parental bondage. Strategies are discussed to handle the stress and fear associated with the inevitable confrontation that arises with the narcissistic parent.

Over-Indulged Children: A Parent's Guide to Mentoring, Dr. John Fogarty. An excellent source for educators who must address the concerns of overindulged students and their parents. The book outlines the differing types of overindulgence and easily allows for recognition of the drain on the emotional reserves of those professionals who attempt to assist in the child's development.

The New Six-Point Plan for Raising Happy, Healthy Children, John Rosemond. This publication provides down-to-earth, logical approaches to parenting and strategies for raising children to prevent and address narcissistic tendencies as they initially form.

References

American Psychiatric Association. (1994). *Diagnostic and statistical manual of mental disorders* (4th ed.). Washington DC: American Psychiatric Association.

Annie's mailbox. (2007, December 6). *Troy Daily News*, p. A8.

Ashmun, J. (2004). *Narcissistic personality disorder (NPD): How to recognize a narcissist*. Retrieved October 17, 2007, from www.halcyon.com/jmashmun/npd/dsm-iv .html

Banerjee, N. (2008, February 26). Poll finds a fluid religious life in U.S. *The New York Times*. Retrieved March 9, 2008, from www.nytimes.com/2008/02/26/ us/26religion.html?_r=1&scp=1&sq=%22poll%20finds%20a%20fluid%20religio us%20life%22&st=cse.

Baumeister, Roy F. (2006). Violent pride: Do people turn violent because of self-hate, or self-love? [Electronic version]. *Scientific American Mind, 17* (4), 54–59.

Bounds, A. (2007, November 14). BVSD nixes title of valedictorian. *Daily Camera Online*. Retrieved December 5, 2007, from http://dailycamera.com/news/2007/ nov/14/bvsd-nixes-title-of-valedictorian/.

Bracey, G. W. (2007, October). Sputnik's gift: The schools as scapegoat. *Principal Leadership (High School Edition)*, pp. 62–64.

Bronson, P. (2007, February 12). How not to talk to your kids: The inverse power of praise. *NewYork Magazine*. Retrieved December 2, 2007, from nymag.com/news/ features/27840.

Brown, N. (2001). *Children of the self-absorbed: A grownup's guide to getting over narcissistic parents*. California: New Harbinger Publications, Inc.

Carey, B. (2002, October 14). The narcissist, unmasked. *Los Angeles Times*. Retrieved December 26, 2007, from http://articles.latimes.com/2002/oct/14/health/ he-narcissism14.

Carey, B. (2007, September 14). Bipolar illness soars as a diagnosis for the young. *The New York Times*. Retrieved March 9, 2008, from http://www.nytimes. com/2007/09/04/health/04psych.html?scp=1&sq=%22bipolar%20illness%20soars %20as%22&st=cse.

Child Development Institute. (n.d.). "Stages of social-emotional development in children and teenagers." Retrieved December 25, 2007, from www.childdevelop mentinfo.com/development/erickson.shtml

"Controversy of the week." (2008, June 13). *The Week*. p. 4.

"DSM-IV multiaxial system (made easy)." (n.d.). *PSYweb.com*. Retrieved December 10, 2007, from http://psyweb.com/Mdisord?DSM_IV/jsp/dsm_iv.jsp.

Ferrero, D. (2005, February). Pathways to reform: Start with values. *The Best of Educational Leadership 2004–2005*, pp. 21–26.

FilingforBankruptcy.Online. (2002-2006). "Statistics about bankruptcy filings." Retrieved February 29, 2008, from www.filingforbankruptcyonline.com/stats.html.

Fogarty, J. (2003). *Over-indulged children: A parent's guide to mentoring*. North Carolina: Liberty Publishing Group.

Fogarty, J. (Speaker). (2008, January). *Overindulged children and conduct disorder: Treating overindulgent families*. Vandalia, Ohio.

Gillespie, C. (2008, July 21). Personal communication.

Goudarzi, S. (2006, September). Area of brain associated with higher-level thinking underused in youths. *LiveScience*. Retrieved December 30, 2007, from www.msnbc. msn.com/id/14738243.

Growing Out of ADHD. (2007, November 30). *The Week*. p. 22.

Heath, C., and Heath, D. (2007). *Made to stick: Why some ideas survive and others die*. New York: Random House Publishing Co.

Hope, J. (2007, March). The great ADHD myth. *The Daily Mail*. Retrieved March 9, 2008, from www.dailymail.co.uk/news/article-441304/The-great-ADHD-myth .html.

Hotchkiss, S. (2002). *Why is it always about you? The seven deadly sins of narcissism*. New York: Free Press.

James, S. D. (2008, February 29). Cheating scandals rock three top-tier high schools. *ABC News*. Retrieved March 31, 2008, from http://abcnews.go.com/ print?id=4362510.

Karnick, S. T. (2007, February). Ideas have consequences: Self-esteem, achievement, and narcissism. *The American Culture*. Retrieved December 6, 2007, from http:// stkarnick.com/blog2/2007/02/ideas_have_consequences_selfes.html.

Kelley, W. (2003). *Common sense: A new conversation about public education*. Bloomington, IN: Xlibris.

Lasch, C. (1979). *The culture of narcissism: American life in an age of diminishing expectations*. New York: W. W. Norton and Company.

Liptak, A. (2008, February 28). 1 in 100 U.S. adults behind bars, new study says. *The New York Times*. Retrieved March 9, 2008, from http://www.nytimes. com/2008/02/28/us/28cnd-prison.html?sq=%221%20in%20100%20u.s.%20adul ts%20behind%20bars%22&st=cse&adxnnl=1&scp=1&adxnnlx=1239724884-i1kX0/34o1zARx1krEHTeg.

Lyons, L. (1995, August). *Public education: A means of affecting character development.* Valdosta, GA: Valdosta State University. Retrieved December 2, 2007, from http://chiron.valdosta.edu/whuitt/files/chardev.html.

McGraw, P. (Host). (2007, October 12). *Dr. Phil Now: Homecoming Shooting* [Television broadcast]. Chicago: Harpo, Inc.

Namka, L. (1997). "You owe me! Children of entitlement." Retrieved April 10, 2009, from www.angriesout.com/teach9.htm.

Noted. (2008, March 14). *The Week.* p. 18.

Riera, M. (2003). *Staying connected to your teenager: How to keep them talking to you and how to hear what they're really saying.* Massachusetts: Perseus Publishing.

Rosemond, J. (1990). *Parent power: A common sense approach to parenting in the 90's and beyond.* Kansas City: Andrews McMeel Publishing.

Rosemond, J. (2000). *Raising a nonviolent child.* Kansas City: Andrews McMeel Publishing.

Rosemond, J. (Speaker). (2003, November). *Parenting by the book.* Huber Heights, Ohio.

Rosemond, J. (2006). *The new six-point plan for raising happy, healthy children.* Kansas City: Andrews McMeel Publishing.

Sacks, D. (2006, January/February). Scenes from the culture clash. *Fast Company,* pp. 73–77.

Sax, L. (2006, March 31). What's happening to boys? *Washington Post.* Retrieved March 10, 2008, from www.washingtonpost.com/wp-dyn/content/article/2006/03/30/AR2006033001241_pf.html

Schencker, L. (2007, November 26). Study: When gauging educators, many parents value student satisfaction over performance. *The Salt Lake Tribune.* Retrieved November 28, 2007, from http://www.sltrib.com/news/ci_7559909.

Sherrill, S. (2001, December 9). Acquired situational narcissism. *New York Times.* Retrieved October 8, 2007, from www.nytimes.com/2001/12/09/magazine/the-year-in-ideas-a-to-z-acquired-situational-narcissism.html.

Spock, B. (2001). *The school years: The emotional and social development of children.* New York: Pocket Books.

Super, J. C. (2005). *The seventies in America: Education in the United States.* Pasadena, CA.: Salem Press, Inc. Retrieved December 2, 2007, from http://salempress.com/Store/samples/seventies_in_america/seventies_in_america_education_in_the_united_states.htm.

Talking points. (2007, October 5). *The Week.* p. 22.

U.S. Department of Education. (2007, August). *Jacob K. Javits gifted and talented students education program.* Retrieved December 9, 2007, from http://www.ed.gov/programs/javits/index.html.

Vaknin, S. (2004, January). Acquired situational narcissism. *Holistic Junction.* Retrieved October 8, 2007, from www.holisticjunction.com/articles/1049.html.

White, J. (2008, January 30). U.S. home foreclosures rise by 75 percent in 2007. *World Socialist Web Site*. Retrieved February 29, 2008, from www.wsws.org/articles/2008/jan2008/home-j30_prn.shtml.

Wooden, J., and Jamison, S. (1997). *A lifetime of observations and reflections on and off the court*. Lincolnwood, IL: Contemporary Publishing Company.

About the Authors

Chad Mason began his career in 1994 after graduating with his B.S.B.A. from Ohio Northern University. He obtained his Master's Degree in Educational Administration in 1999 from the University of Dayton and then received his superintendent's licensure in 2000. He is currently completing his residency at the University of Dayton in the Educational Administration Doctoral Program.

Mr. Mason has nearly sixteen years' experience in education, with eight of those in the administrative ranks. During this time, he has served as a high school business teacher, a varsity girls' basketball coach, an academic team advisor, a high school assistant principal, a middle school assistant principal, and a high school principal.

He is currently a member of the Ohio Association of Secondary School Administrators and the National Association of Secondary School Administrators.

Mr. Mason is married and has one son. He and his family currently reside in Troy, Ohio, where he serves as assistant principal of an area middle school.

Karen Brackman graduated in 1987 from Miami University in Oxford, Ohio, with a B.S. in Education certified to teach secondary English, reading, and mathematics. She earned her Masters Degree in English Education in 1995 and her counseling certificate in 2002, both from the University of Dayton.

Mrs. Brackman has been employed by two different districts in her twenty-one years of educational experience. The first school was a middle school in suburban northwestern Illinois; the second, a rural district in southwestern Ohio. In addition to various extracurricular positions, she has taught both middle school and high school English, and she currently serves as a high school guidance counselor.

She is married and has two children—one daughter and one son. She and her family reside near Dayton, Ohio.